Praise for *Sun Tzu:*

"A unique and engaging blend of timeless wisdom and practical strategies."

Roger Dow, SVP Global Sales,
Marriott International, Inc.

"How to apply the Master's principles to the modern selling battlefield!"

Art Jacobs, President & CEO
Valkyrie Management Corp.

"Drawing on extensive sales experience and comprehensive knowledge, the Michaelsons offer a unique perspective of relationship selling."

Eugene Johnson, Professor of Marketing
University of Rhode Island

"A must for everyone trying to excel."

Arvydas Strumskis, CEO
VisSTRATA Ltd., Lithuania

"The Michaelsons show how valuable Sun Tzu's teachings are in the critical area of selling."

C. J. Kurtz, President
The Kappa Group

SUN TZU

Strategies
for Selling

How to Use The Art of War
to Build Lifelong Customer Relationships

Gerald A. Michaelson

with

Steven W. Michaelson

McGraw-Hill

New York Chicago San Francisco Lisbon London
Madrid Mexico City Milan New Delhi San Juan
Seoul Singapore Sydney Toronto

McGraw-Hill A Division of The McGraw-Hill Companies Copyright ©2004 by Gerald A. Michaelson. All rights reserved. Printed in the United States of America. Except as permitted under the United States Copyright Act of 1976, no part of this publication may be reproduced or distributed in any form or by any means, or stored in a data base or retrieval system, without the prior written permission of the publisher.

1 2 3 4 5 6 7 8 9 0   AGM/AGM   0 9 8 7 6 5 4 3

ISBN 0-07-142730-9

Translations from the Chinese by Pan Jiabin and Liu Ruxian.

McGraw-Hill books are available at special quantity discounts to use as premiums and sales promotions, or for use in corporate training programs. For more information, please write to the Director of Special Sales, Professional Publishing, McGraw-Hill, Two Penn Plaza, New York, NY 10121-2298. Or contact your local bookstore.

Library of Congress Cataloging-in-Publication Data

Michaelson, Gerald A.
   Sun Tzu strategies for selling : how to use the art of war to build
lifelong customer relationships / by Gerald A. Michaelson.
     p. cm.
   ISBN 0-07-142730-9 (alk. paper)
  1. Selling. 2. Sunzi, 6th cent. B.C. Sunzi bing fa. I. Title.
  HF5438.25.M5373 2004
  658.85—dc22

                           2003018816

This book is printed on recycled, acid-free paper containing a minimum of 50% recycled de-inked fiber.

CONTENTS

CONTENTS

*Dedicated to honor the loving memory of
the finest sales professional we have known,
Alexander Knute Michaelson*

Preface

Question: What can a book titled *The Art of War* teach us about the profession of selling?

Answer: We can learn much because the book is really about winning without conflict—the crux of successful selling.

Sun Tzu's book was written to help emperors think about winning without fighting. Imagine that! One of the oldest books in history is about win-win thinking—the heart of selling. A win by the salesperson must be a win by the customer.

The Art of War was designed to help emperors:

Win without fighting.
—or—
Win if they must engage in conflict.

The same concepts help sales professionals:

Win before engaging in a competitive battle.
—or—
Win when selling against competition.

The underlying concepts for winning have not changed. We can go back to Sun Tzu for fundamentals and take this simple wisdom forward to modern times to apply it to success in selling.

Selling is the ultimate diplomacy in the business engagement—all activities exist to support it.

Traditionally, selling involved the expertise of a single individual—as Arthur Miller wrote, "a man way out there in the blue, riding on a smile and a shoeshine."

Today, selling is the lifelong vocation of men and women working in teams to coordinate services for customers. Even

PREFACE

when there is no formal sales team, informal teamwork is often required.

When Sun Tzu's concepts are applied to selling, everyone benefits because almost everything we do involves selling. Knowledge of the strategies and tactics of selling can enhance business and personal life.

Our objective is to use Sun Tzu's timeless wisdom to crystallize and reinforce concepts for success in selling. Although nothing is really new, everything can be seen in a new way. The old works; integrate the new, and the result is better.

Book One uses selected passages from *The Art of War* to focus on key sales concepts. Within Book One:

Part I organizes personal strengths.
Part II focuses on planning.
Part III initiates action.
Part IV structures the successful sales relationship.
Part V offers the wisdom of practical experience.

Book Two is the complete translation of Sun Tzu's *The Art of War*, which was discovered by the author on a visit to China.

Our commentary on applying the timeless wisdom of Sun Tzu is based on years of practical experience in working with customers in every state and many foreign lands. We have drawn from career experiences in selling and buying.

Your success in applying Sun Tzu's timeless wisdom is our success. Our every wish is for your continued success.

Gerald A. Michaelson
Steven W. Michaelson
SunTzu@TeamMichaelson.com

BOOK ONE

APPLYING
TIMELESS WISDOM

Part I

Personal Strength
Wisdom

Sun Tzu wrote *The Art of War* on bamboo strips about 500 B.C. This classic of Eastern military strategy focuses on "winning without fighting." In contrast, much of Western strategy focuses on "fighting big battles" as the way to win.

Although the timeless wisdom of the underlying strategies of selling has not changed, the tactical execution has changed.

THE NEW RELATIONSHIPS

The business world is shifting from dealing with the conflict that can exist between the interests of buyer and seller to seeking a continual consensus.

This consensus is most visible in business-to-business relationships in the form of partnership agreements in which both organizations share resources focused on a common goal.

In direct-to-customer relationships, this search for buying consensus can be seen in brand loyalty programs and levels of quality that delight customers.

Many sales professionals are transitioning from soliciting business from many potential customers to a new role of managing and facilitating strong relationships with a select group of existing customers.

In all selling situations, the emphasis is on building and maintaining a long-term relationship. It's not that you don't want customers to look elsewhere to buy; it's that you want the total relationship with the customer to be so strong customers do not even *think* of looking elsewhere to buy. The key issue is not how to make the sale; rather, it is establishing a relationship that builds repeat business.

To state the issue simply: The sales process is the lifelong relationship with the customer.

TEAMWORK

In the new world of global competition, the salesperson's strength alone is not enough. What wins is the power of the team focused on the customer.

The sales professional's role is as a member (or leader) of a sales team focused on the customer.

Your strength is greatest when the forces of your team are marshaled to win sales.

Teamwork in sales, as in sports, is the sum of individual efforts working toward a common goal. Just as some ballplayers do better in certain positions, so it is with business teams. Applying the football metaphor to business, appropriate designations for team members could be coach, quarterback, center, and receiver.

YOUR EVER-CHANGING ROLE

As team members, we need to have the skills to adapt to different roles. Every sales opportunity is different, and every sales opportunity requires us to use our skills in different ways.

In the 1990s, a famous football player, Dion Sanders, had skills in a variety of positions. Sanders returned punts, played cornerback on defense, and was sometimes an offensive receiver. His underlying strength in every position was speed.

When playing different positions, Sanders utilized his skills in a different manner. On offense, he used his speed to run his preassigned pattern and break away from the coverage. On defense, Sanders used speed to break for a tackling opportunity at a moment of his own choosing.

Likewise, if we are continually selling the same way and not changing, we are not keeping up with the competitive world. If we do not present new ideas and concepts to our customers, our competitors will offer those new ideas. The only way we can stay in first place is to keep changing.

Here are several examples of how the sales role is changing. And these changing scenarios are being repeated in many business relationships.

- Manufacturers are drastically reducing the number of suppliers. This means that a lot of salespeople are losing customers. If you are not on the preferred supplier list, you are on the outside looking in.
- Suppliers who survive the cut have found that an entirely new relationship style is needed to mobilize their corporate resources to serve the customer.
- As Wal-Mart's business grew, Procter & Gamble reorganized its entire sales structure serving this customer. Years ago, a handful of salespeople traveled to Wal-Mart headquarters in Bentonville, Arkansas. Today, a large cadre of P&G people live near Bentonville in order to provide the best possible service to Wal-Mart.

In the emerging new sales paradigm, the emphasis is on teams that nurture long-term relationships with customers. The biggest difficulty in understanding the new sales paradigm is that the old paradigm of one-on-one selling still works in some circumstances.

When a change occurs in a business paradigm, it doesn't mean that the new paradigm is entirely new. What is true about the paradigm has always been true. It's just that a significant number of people have begun to understand that a new methodology works better.

To say that teams are a better way to sell or that long-term relationships are important doesn't mean that the fundamentals of selling have changed. New paradigm selling simply recognizes the situational importance of people working as a team to develop a long-term service relationship with a customer.

This situation is much like the change in style for winning the high jump. The scissors and the roll have long been superseded by the Fosbury Flop. The old method still works, but it does not win competitive championships.

To better understand how to implement new paradigm selling, start with your biggest customer and think about what you would do if this were your only customer. Have a team conference on the subject, write a plan, and implement it. Then proceed to the next-biggest customer, and the next.

You will find that what you must do to "marry" one customer is similar for all customers. This active process can be quite different from what you are doing today to serve these customers.

Going through this exercise will do much to increase your understanding of your changing role.

THE QUALITY OF YOUR PROFESSIONAL ROLE

The coin of quality has two sides. One side is the quality built into the product or service. The other side is the quality of the sales experience as perceived by the customer.

Too often, we think only of the first dimension of quality—that which is intrinsic to the product or service itself. This leads to thinking that quality is the responsibility of someone else in the organization. The customer's perception of quality *is* the responsibility of the sales professional. This responsibility includes everything we do in our relationship with the customer as well as efforts to improve the performance quality of the product or service we sell.

As the person most frequently in contact with the customer, the salesperson has the responsibility of acting as a data conduit from and to the customer. Our credibility with information receivers gets tarnished when we transmit only opinions. What counts are data. In some cases, it may be prudent to present statistical charts of how the product or process is performing. In

7

other cases, it may be helpful to present data in an organized manner.

In the military, headquarters has a problem with field reports that describe "heavy shelling" or "intense fire" because these terms have a different meaning for different people. A similar problem exists in business when field reports are too general, such as those indicating problems with "late deliveries" or "too many backorders." To get better results for our customers, data must be quantified by stating, for example, "how many times the delivery was late and by how many days." Collect the data over a period of time—at least 30 days.

Data are useful not only within our own organization but also in discussions with the customer. Consider this case: The salesperson was about to lose the customer because the product wasn't performing to specification. Our sales professional convened his associates, collected the data on the product performance, and presented them to the customer. The data proved that the customer was correct—the product wasn't performing to specification. The customer was so impressed with this frank admission and accurate presentation of the problem he agreed to work with the supplier to improve performance. Think about the improved perception of personal integrity that must have accompanied this interchange.

The customer wants performance, and that means no excuses now or in the future. Excuses are best avoided by creating circumstances that reduce the possibility of failure. It has been well said, "There are only two types of situations. Those where you have a good excuse for not doing it right and those where it is done right!" Plan on giving no excuses!

The performance of *the entire relationship* is how the customer rates the quality of his or her experience. This "total overview" is a vital dimension of quality. Think about it: You do not return to restaurants if either the food *or* service is awful. Poor performance in either one will keep you from coming back. So it is in selling. Poor service performance can cancel the value of an excellent product, and excellent service seldom rescues a poor product.

To achieve the highest level of quality for customers, you must have quality relationships within your organization. This requires the following type of relationship thinking:

- *Internal customers.* Everyone delivers a product or service to someone else. That someone else is a customer.
- *Involvement.* Everyone is involved in quality because everyone has a contribution to make.
- *Teamwork.* Input is sought from teams, and contributions are made by teams. Individualism is out. Teamwork is in.

The more you understand about how quality is achieved, the better you are able to sell your product or service in meaningful terms to the customer.

Your personal level of service quality is important because a major cause of customer dissatisfaction with the processes associated with the sale and delivery of the product.

Quality service in sales is everything we do that touches the customer: It's the way we answer the phone. It's the depth of knowledge we have of our product or service, customer, market, industry, and the world. It's keeping the promises we make. It's doing our homework and being prepared. It's being on time. It's being thorough. It's being of service. It's the entire professionalism of our conduct.

We are the primary producers of the service quality of our own sales process. If we are not continually working on improving sales quality, then sales quality is deteriorating. Continuous improvement in everything we do is the price for getting and keeping a reputation for quality.

Sales quality starts with finding out what the customer wants. What the customer wants keeps changing; the road to sales quality has no end. Quite simply, quality is whatever the customer says it is.

YOUR STRENGTH

Your personal strength is much like that of a building. First, we must rise from a solid foundation of who we are, what we know, and our beliefs and values.

The second element of strength of any structure is a solid framework. Your self-knowledge and self-direction are the framework that determines your strength.

1
Meet the Enemy

We have met the enemy and he is us!
—"General" Pogo

 Pogo, the cartoon strip philosopher, declared to his friend Albert the Alligator, "We have met the enemy and he is us!" Sun Tzu probably had too large an ego to make this kind of statement. But Pogo had it right. Our first and most important battle is with ourselves.

Knowing that too often "the enemy is us" helps in understanding the most important component for success. To make sure that you are not the enemy of your own success, seek counsel from someone who is interested in your success but not directly involved in the planning or execution of the process.

We are blind to our weaknesses and condemned to repeat our errors unless we seek outside advice that will clearly point out where we are fighting ourselves.

Beware of the tendency to hear only what we want to hear and to use that information to stroke our convictions. This process can become a never-ending spiral. It has been wisely said that when a person becomes centered on himself or herself, any risk is too great, because either success or failure will destroy him or her.

In military and business, organizations that do the best have the best leadership. When I asked my sales organization what

11

branch stores in a specific chain were the best, it readily identified the best stores. When I asked what made these stores outstanding, all readily volunteered that the branch manager made the difference. When I asked what made the difference between a good- and poor-performing sales territory, they got the message. What makes the difference is us.

Be as critical of yourself as you are of others. When you have truly met the enemy, go to the head of the class. Your success is a product of you. It's very important that you like yourself and what you do each day. Be committed to your faith, your family, and your company—in that order. Develop good habits.

Vince Lombardi is held in esteem as a winning professional football coach and as a fine individual. During Lombardi's tenure as a football coach for the Green Bay Packers, he lost only one postseason game—the first one. Then he coached the team to nine play-off victories in a row.

Because he fined his players heavily for being late to meetings, players arrived on time. "Lombardi time" came to be understood as arriving early for an appointment. A great idea for every sales professional. Here are a few other Lombardi principles to consider:

- Be both industrious and meticulous in your analysis. Take notes. Organize and file.
- Visual education is much better than just talking to people.
- Make no little plans. Make big plans.
- If you don't strive to innovate, someone will come up with something better.
- The reach should always exceed the grasp.
- Admit it when you make a mistake.
- Battles are won primarily in the hearts of men (and women).
- Success is 75 percent mental.

- Be willing to take a chance. *Throw the ball!*
- The measure of a person is how he or she meets failure.
- If you could have won, you should have won.

TIMELESS WISDOM

Each business professional who is selling anything determines the acceptance of a service product called "me." Aim for world class goals. You and your customers deserve the best. Be the very best.

2
Knowledge Leads to Victory

Know the enemy and know yourself,
and your victory will never be endangered.
—Sun Tzu

 Knowledgeable preparation is everything. Successful selling requires a lifetime of learning about your customers, products, services, industry, and the art and science of making sales.

The required knowledge extends to every area of our being and our business universe. Every man and woman is accountable for adequate knowledge of the components that affect his or her success or failure.

SELF-KNOWLEDGE

Know your strengths. Know your weaknesses. Although it is important to recognize and improve weaknesses, the best investments are in reinforcing our strengths.

Getting better at what you do best brings the best results.

It has been well said that it is not that history repeats itself but, rather, that the errors of history repeat themselves. Avoid the trap of repeating the same mistakes.

Understanding yourself is one of the basic components of personality profile systems like the Myers-Briggs Type Indicator (MBTI). Self-knowledge can be very useful in determining how to communicate with your customer.

Personality profiles help us understand our own personality preferences. The more we know about our own preferences, the easier it is to understand the personality preferences of others. Greater self-knowledge can help you correctly read your customer and adapt to his or her personality.

For example, MBTI states that people have a preference for either thinking or feeling when making decisions. Thinkers tend to decide using logic; feelers decide based on emotion. Although most of us employ both logic and emotion in the decision-making process, each of us has a preference for one style or the other.

On a deeper level, some thinkers have a sensing preference— that is, they prefer a list of accurate facts. Other thinkers have an intuitive preference—that is, they want an overview of options so they can determine how to use the product or service.

If unaware of different decision-making preferences, we assume that everyone makes decisions the same way we do. Understanding that different decision-making preferences exist makes us more aware of the need to observe our customer's preference. Obviously, a presentation loaded with logic can be lost on a customer who tends to decide based on emotion.

BUSINESS KNOWLEDGE

The People's Republic of China army regulations state, "Every commander must organize reconnaissance within his unit's zone of activities." Your goal is to know more than anyone else about your industry and area of responsibility. This knowledge starts with reading trade publications and news sources and continues through every source of input. The search is always for new opportunities.

Knowing is not enough. Where your product or service is sold by sales organizations, you must train these people. The best training is interactive. In sales meetings, use questions to elicit information. One of my favorite sessions is when the leader simply identifies a product or service and asks, "What are the important things to sell?" When a participant responds with a feature, ask about the benefit. Continue asking until the group runs out of responses, and you will find that you have a few more benefits to add. Everyone learns, including the meeting leader, who gets new features and benefits to use in his or her next meeting. Attention level is high because people are actively participating.

When your customers are business executives, think about training programs that can help them be more successful. Bring a group together to meet with experts in various management areas such as information systems, accounting, taxes, human resources management, and recruiting. Knowing how to hire and grow good people is the key ingredient to the success of any business. The best organizations have the best people. Providing this professional knowledge is a service that will make you a more valuable resource to your customers. Equally important, the knowledge you gain from these sessions will be useful to you in your career growth.

CUSTOMER KNOWLEDGE

The successful sale is made *before* meeting the customer, not *when* meeting the customer.

Customer knowledge is one of the sciences of selling. Doing the required research is a hallmark of the sales professional. The required research extends beyond general business knowledge to specific knowledge of your customers and their businesses. Think about thinking like a customer: Put yourself in the customer's shoes.

Although recognizing the need for customer knowledge is not new, the phrase *customer relationship management (CRM)* is new in sales and marketing. It emphasizes the importance of personal knowledge of your customers and relating with them on the basis of that knowledge. You can never know enough about your customer. Take notes after each meeting. Keep a file and review it regularly.

Downstream in many sales channels are several customers, all of whom must be satisfied. We need some level of knowledge about why these customers buy. In business-to-business selling, you win when you know more about why your customer's customers buy than your customer does.

TIMELESS WISDOM

Know yourself, your industry, and your customers, and your business will never be endangered.

3
Be Professional

 The professional has it in *his or her power to control success* because he or she understands and applies a body of scientific knowledge. It has been well said that selling is a trade for the ignorant and a science for the professional.

The word *sell* is derived from the Icelandic word *selja* and the Anglo-Saxon word *syllan*, meaning "to give" or "to serve." Selling is focusing on serving customers in the finest way possible. Those who serve best win.

When interviewing a potential salesperson, one of the questions I ask is, "What are the last five books you have read?" I am not looking for specific titles but rather for a type of book. I want people who are reading books on self-improvement, the sales profession, or their industry. I want to hire people who are good and who are investing time in getting better.

I learned about asking about the last five books read when reading how Adm. Hyman Rickover interviewed recruits for his nuclear submarine program. The response can reveal interesting personal qualities.

One summer morning I interviewed an aspiring sales recruit dressed in sartorial splendor. He wore a brown-and-yellow-checked suit with a matching brown tie and yellow shirt. When I asked how he learned how to sell, he responded brightly, "Mr. Michaelson, I am a naturally born salesman." Right then and there, he lost. I believe that we are all "naturally born" and that's all. Some people may have more "talent" in the arts. However, professional skills are honed through study and practice. People who think that their sales skills are "naturally born" will not focus on self-improvement. Their personal growth will be stalled.

If you could read a book a day, you could never read all the books written on the profession of selling. Not having time to read is not an excuse. Much of today's selling information can also be acquired though audio and video means. As a sales manager, I provided my salespeople with recordings of sales presentations. By learning during a time period that would have been downtime, we upgraded our professional skills.

Not taking the time to learn how to get better is much like the woodcutter who said he was so busy chopping wood he did not have time to sharpen his ax. Take time to get better. Have a plan to sharpen your professional edge.

THE ART AND SCIENCE OF THE PROFESSIONAL

Generals say that "war is an art served by many sciences." Similarly, we can say that selling is "an art served by many sciences." As an art, excellence in the sales profession requires practice and more practice. As a science, excellence in the sales profession requires the constant study of a body of knowledge in order to continuously improve.

Selling is not the hard science associated with physical laws in which actions consistently produce the same reactions; rather, it is the soft science associated with psychological and social laws, in which prescribed actions increase the probability of certain reactions. For example, the basic process of the soft science of selling can be derived from the acronym AIDA. That is, the first step is to get the customers Attention, next build Interest in what you are selling, then develop the Desire to own, and the final Action step is getting the order.

The professional understands the importance of taking no chances with the controllable elements of the sale (such as being on time) because there are so many uncontrollable elements.

The professional understands the psychology of the selling situation and takes care of the little things that make a difference. Professionals know when to make the choice between getting ready (preparation) and getting going (action). They know that the greatest odds for success lie on the side of action; when we do something, we tend to become master of the situation.

SET HIGH STANDARDS

Standards are conditions we set for performance. For Sun Tzu, standards would flow from his admonition "Adhere to the laws and regulations."

Set high standards for your own performance and have high expectations of those with whom you work. The higher the goal, the greater will be the achievement.

When we plan for low levels of performance, that's what we get. Set high standards and achieve more. Consider surveying your customers about your performance. Their opinion is the only one that really matters. You will get the most honest answers if this survey is done by an independent agency that guarantees not to reveal the origin of the responses. A good survey technique is to have the customer respond concerning a questionnaire about the performance of all the people who call on the organization.

HIGH BUSINESS STANDARDS

Simple standards for meeting clients can be a firm handshake and a look in the eye. Presentation standards can be guidelines for meeting-site preparation, handouts, use of visuals, and everything that affects success. Ethical standards require honesty and integrity.

On my portable computer is a checklist of standards to review prior to every presentation. The list includes checking the lights, testing the overhead projector, making sure that I have a spare bulb, locating the temperature control, having pens and blank transparencies, checking the line of sight from fringe seats, doing a final check of the visuals, and knowing the vital business statistics of key participants.

At Baldrige-award-winning Ritz-Carlton hotels, the standard for responding to a customer's request is words like "Certainly" or "My pleasure." "Sure," "OK," and "Yeah" are out. If the inquiry requires directions, the standard is to escort the guest to the location—positively no pointing and saying, "It's that way." I noticed this same standard at a fine restaurant. It was probably "stolen" from Ritz-Carlton. This kind of "theft" is OK. Just be sure to "steal" only from the best.

At Delta Airlines, the standard is that after pulling up to the gate, the pilot must stand in the cockpit doorway and thank passengers as they exit.

At Federal Express, the standard is that all incoming calls must be answered on or before the third ring. A friend told me that when the phone was not answered on the fourth ring, he hung up because he thought he had dialed the wrong number.

These examples of standards are the way corporations ensure that a consistently friendly face is presented to all customers.

HIGH STANDARDS
FOR PERSONAL CONDUCT

In the everyday world, the mark of a real pro is our behavior when we are not selling. Professional behavior isn't something turned off and on like a light switch. The professional is a professional all of the time.

Of course, smoking on the customer's premises is out. When calling at a place of business, never park in spaces that might be convenient for customers. When the client takes a phone call, leave the office. That way you show courtesy for his or her privacy and avoid the embarrassment of being asked to leave.

Don't say the wrong things, and don't use the wrong words when you say the right things. Sex, religion, and racial comments do not belong in any business discussions. Period. Foul language is out. Way out. Period. Make sure your jokes are wholesome and appropriate.

Don't discuss your competitor. You certainly don't want to say anything good about your competitor's company—and saying something bad can backfire. If you say anything, use faint praise like, "They are good people." You won't win by dragging other people down.

Avoid "No"—particularly at the beginning of a sentence or in response to a question. Suggest alternatives. Talk about what you can do. At an airport counter, I did not have a document the agent needed. The agent didn't say "No. I can't ticket you unless you get the required document." Instead, she said, "Yes, I can ticket you when you get the required document." Note how the word "yes" can put a positive spin on a refusal.

"You'll have to . . ." is a deadly phrase to a customer. The customer doesn't "have to" do anything. Try a phrase such as "The best thing to do is . . ." or "Yes, you can be taken care of if . . . ."

Use good words. Instead of saying "cost" or "payment," say "investment." For example, instead of "How much did you want to pay?" ask, "How much are you thinking of investing?" Avoid words like "pay." For example, the question "Did you want monthly or annual premiums?" completely leaves out the word "pay."

Instead of saying "signature" or "sign," say "OK" or "approve." Remember that we've been taught never to sign anything.

The right language is both what we say and what we don't say.

No sales professional works in a vacuum. The standards and expectations we set for ourselves and our team members have much to do with the results that will be achieved. Aim for the stars.

Successful selling often involves successful presentations. Enroll in a Toastmasters club to improve your speaking ability.

TIMELESS WISDOM

Act like a professional. Think like a professional. Be a professional. Achievement of excellence is a requirement, not an option.

Knowledge of both the art and the science of the sales profession is the price of entry to success.

4
Occupy the High Ground

In battles and maneuvering,
all armies prefer high ground to low.
—Sun Tzu

 The high ground may be an ethical position, a product or service superiority, or contacts with high-level decision makers. All high-ground positions are desirable.

THE ETHICAL HIGH GROUND

You want to be on the ethical high ground *and* be perceived as being on it. Doing what is morally right always pays off in the long run. It takes a long time to build a good reputation; a single action can ruin that reputation.

You may not be able to control the conditions determining performance of your product. You *can* control your personal reputation for trust, integrity, and service. These three words are linked. Take away the reputation for service, and the other two are gone. In turn, trust and integrity are earned by giving prompt, dependable service. Be reliable. Do what you say you will do when you say you will do it. If you cannot meet a deadline, call and advise the other person prior to the deadline date.

It has been well said: "If you do not have integrity, nothing else matters. If you have integrity, nothing else matters." Build trusting relationships with everyone in your network.

THE PRODUCT OR SERVICE HIGH GROUND

Superiority in product or service performance brings rich rewards. If improvement is needed to get your company's product or service to the high ground of superiority, generate the feedback—send data. Your own personal service level must be world class; anything less is off the high ground and headed for the swamp.

THE PERSONAL CONTACT HIGH GROUND

Whenever possible, initiate your contacts with a new prospect at the highest possible level. Even if you do not get in the door at the top of the organization, you will be directed to the right department. When the link to the buyer comes from a high level, you are more likely to get favorable attention and a sale.

When you start too low, you always have the problem of being perceived as going over someone's head. When you start at the top and have not met that "someone," you are less likely to be perceived as going over his or her head.

Selling from the bottom up is a long climb. Selling from the top down gets results much faster.

When you know the top, don't forget the bottom. The guy at the loading dock or the receptionist in the office can be a great source of information. A college sports coach with a great reputation for recruiting outstanding players told me about the importance of the receptionist in the high school office in providing information on student athletes.

Beware: Starting at the top has pitfalls and dangers. How the "top" introduces you to decision makers further down the line is critical to success.

Sometimes, the senior manager will recommend the product or service during the introduction. More often, top managers delegate complete decision-making authority and hold the team accountable for results. In these instances, the introduction is more of a suggestion—an opening of the door of opportunity. The suggestion may be embraced or rejected because subordinates fear that

- The relationship is with the top manager, not with them.
- They will lose control because of your influence with the top manager.
- You will be a spy, and report failures.

Avoid these pitfalls by taking the following positive actions after the introduction:

- Don't overplay your relationship with top management. Be humble. Build support for the front-line decision maker.
- Handle all decision-maker contacts with the same respect and urgency you would give to the top managers.
- Make your relationship with top management a benefit to the decision maker. Help strengthen the front line's position. Make the subordinates look like heroes and find subtle ways to let them know you are making them look like heroes.

Just because you had a high-level sponsor introduce you into the organization does not mean that everyone likes you or the situation. As one senior buyer said about a president who had a habit of personally referring vendors to the purchasing staff, "I've never seen the president write a purchase order."

THE MENTAL HIGH GROUND

Seek the mental high ground. If we think we can, we will. When we think we can, we tend to do the things that help us be achievers. A positive attitude toward success helps us achieve goals. If we have a good attitude, negative events do not adversely affect us. We see this wonderful situation in people who are "always up."

Success flows from the high ground of positive thinking. Take a mental journey through a previous positive experience. Get things working in your mind, and you will find things working in the real world.

Positive attitudes and experiences are self-reinforcing. Successful sales experiences generate a level of confidence that guides you through problems. When things are tough, focus your thoughts on prior positive experiences or move into the positive-action mode by making a few more sales calls. You will be amazed at the results.

Positive attitudes generate positive experiences, and positive experiences generate positive attitudes. These reinforcements of success don't just magically appear; we have to be our own generator.

Prior to a selling situation, stop and mentally pump yourself up. Imagine that you have an air pump and mentally go through the process of pumping air into your shoes. Feel the exhilaration surging through your body. Then, walk on air into the opportunity, but only when you are well prepared.

Life is full of reruns. Repeat the script for successful experiences, and rewrite the script for unsuccessful experiences.

Team up with successful people who will share their positive experiences. Keeping pumped up keeps your customer pumped up. Enthusiasm is contagious.

A flock of geese will fly faster in formation than a single goose flying alone. Winners flock and seek people and situations from which they can get positive experiences. Move from small successes to big ones. Before attempting the big sale, I do a test run. Whenever I have a new product or program to sell, I call on a smaller, friendly account to experience success and fine-tune my approach before tackling the big one.

TIMELESS WISDOM

Aim for the high ground. When you find something that works well, ride it all the way to the bank. Success is a wonderful self-reinforcing experience.

5
Be an Expert

Those skilled in war can make themselves invincible.
Know the weather and know the ground,
and your victory will be complete.
—Sun Tzu

 Knowing your product or service isn't good enough. You must go beyond being "one of many." What makes you and your personal service invincible is being an expert *and* being recognized as an expert. Your objective must be to know more about "it" than anyone else in the world.

In every professional field are practitioners who have general knowledge and specialists who have a depth of knowledge in a specific field. The narrower, and more advanced, the field of specialization, the greater are the opportunities.

Set a goal and a date for reaching that goal. Identify the requirements for achieving expertise. Develop your plan. Write it down. It's not so much a case of "if you build it, they will come" as it is "if you build it, you will achieve your goals." Focus on "what you must do," and the "what you will be" will come as a result.

Circumstances may cause you to change your goal. That's OK; set a new one. What is important is to be goal-oriented. Goals are the engines that deliver energy.

Our goal is a moving target that keeps us motivated and directed toward success. Reaching the goal is not nearly as important as the activity of trying to reach the goal. The value is in striving for expertise.

TIMELESS WISDOM

Develop your personal plan of action and get started. Be enthusiastic. Immerse yourself in the world. Enjoy the trip. Life is fun.

6
Understand Selling as a Process

The art of war may be summarized into five steps.
—Sun Tzu

 The master's five steps are a process. Engineers have long conceptualized the way work is done as a process. A *process* is the systematic (step-by-step) way in which a result is achieved.

In selling, this process is not rigid in the sense that a prepared script must be followed. It is rigid in the sense that following a certain series of steps increases the odds of success.

Within the macroprocess of selling are microprocesses such as prospecting, qualifying, presenting, demonstrating, and closing—to name a few.

Success in selling is not being lucky or having talent. It is understanding and applying selling as a process. When we understand selling as a process, we are able to improve the process.

For example, here is a process for greeting a prospect in his or her office:

1. Smile and extend a friendly greeting. Shake hands, if appropriate, and look the prospect in the eye.

2. Glance around and find something to admire or comment on that begins a cordial conversation. Get your signals from pictures on the wall or items on the desk that indicate a special hobby or interest.
3. Select a seat alongside, rather than across from, the prospect. Avoid a position in which incoming light makes it difficult to determine the prospect's facial expressions.
4. Friendly preliminaries are great, but keep them short.
5. Ask the prospect a general question about his or her business needs. One more time, it's not what you have to sell that's important; it's what the customer wants and needs that is key.

This simple microprocess is a component of the larger process of selling.

The next process step is to explore needs and find out how you can fill those needs.

Understanding selling as a process is fundamental to knowing how to achieve success. Examining the sale as a process enables you to replicate success and plan improvements. Every sales process can be outlined or flowcharted. Diagramming the activity helps in understanding that process. The more thoroughly each step in the process is dissected and flowcharted, the easier it is to discover how to improve the process.

The manner in which you control the total presentation experience establishes the competitive superiority of your product or service with the customer.

When we fail, our normal tendency is to work on improving the last step in the process. Usually we think that our closing tactics are at fault; this is often not the case. The best results in process improvement are achieved when you work upstream. For example:

• The step of preparing a list of questions to ask during the sale can have a positive effect on the entire process.

- The relationship you establish early in the meeting can be vital to winning the customer's trust and acceptance of your proposition.

The close is simply a natural result of doing the right things in every step of the sales process.

TIMELESS WISDOM

In all of life, success in the process produces the results. If you work the process, the results will come.

7

Be Organized— Have a System

Order or disorder depends on organization:

Compare the five constant factors.
Make the following seven comparisons.
Five points in which victory may be predicted.
—Sun Tzu

Sun Tzu continually develops lists of key points—a method of organizing thinking that we can adopt.

The first step in sales homework is collecting and organizing information. Not all information is useful. An overload of information can make it difficult to separate the useful from the useless. Knowledge is power only when collected in a systematized manner.

DEVELOP A SYSTEM

The portable computer is an important productivity tool. Spend time immediately after each sales call recording information in the following useful categories:

- *Relationship information.* Personal information about the customer.

- *Business information.* Facts you have learned about your customer and his or her business.
- *Action items.* Your current to-do list, which is a result of the meeting.
- *Parking lot.* Future actions.

Have a section in your computer where you keep notes from seminars and books you have read. Use the power of computer software to organize customer information for easy retrieval.

The information on my laptop computer goes everywhere I go. I'm not smart enough to remember everything I've read or heard. Before meeting customers and making presentations, I browse through my rich personal database, reviewing and absorbing information that helps with my business. The laptop is a great productivity tool because it provides access to volumes of data. The Internet connects you to the world of information about your customers.

Have a system for recording your personal to-do list, phone calls, and notes. I like a blank, hard-cover record book—the kind you can purchase at a bookstore. Some people use an electronic personal data assistant (PDA) to record phone numbers and addresses and to key in customer data. Others use a daily organizer notebook that can be purchased at an office supply store.

Any system works. Writing on scraps of paper is not a system. Be sure to make photocopies of your personal contact list or, when using the computer, back up the file.

My briefcase has several pockets. Each pocket always contains the same items—always. That way I can check contents easily, and seldom do I leave something behind.

BE A NOTE TAKER

Here are three good reasons for taking notes:

- Writing it down helps us remember. When making promises to your customer, do not rely on your memory. Write it down.

- Writing it down impresses the customer. When the customer sees you write it down, he or she knows it is important to you. Also, the customer has a higher level of confidence that action will be taken. This action helps protect your integrity when someone in your response chain drops the ball. The customer is more likely to believe that you did not forget—after all, he or she saw you write it down.
- Writing it down helps organize thinking. Tom Monahan of Domino's Pizza fame continually takes notes on a yellow pad. The pads are filed away and often never looked at again. The purpose of the note taking is to help think things through.

TIMELESS WISDOM

The key is not how much information has been acquired but, rather, how much of the information is organized so that it can be useful.

8
Get Better
and Better

*It is a doctrine of war
that we must have made our position invincible.*
—Sun Tzu

 We either get better or get worse. We either grow
or decay.

A friend whose duties included being a member of the Wal-
Mart board of directors purchases the tapes of conferences he
can't attend and listens to them while driving in his car.

I record my presentations and workshops on sales and
marketing so I can listen to them while en route to another presentation. When listening to a recording made years ago, it's
amazing how many ideas I am reminded of that had been long
forgotten.

Go to every conference you can. Join several professional
organizations and attend their meetings regularly. Although
many speakers may add little to your base of knowledge, an
occasional gem will deliver an overwhelming wealth of information or ideas. These few treasures make the time investment
worthwhile.

DEVELOP YOUR OWN
IMPROVEMENT STAFF

Here are steps you can take to seek advice from successful people:

- *Develop a coach in every customer's organization.* This is a person interested in the success of your company who will tell you what's happening and why at your customer's business. He or she can help you identify threats and opportunities. Clearly identifying who is the coach in a customer's business is a key component of the selling style of successful salespeople. Be an active proponent of working with the coach in every customer's business.
- *Find a wise guru.* Select someone you know who is not connected to your job. Enlist this person as a resource when you want feedback from outside your organization.
- *Solicit an internal coach.* Your coach inside your company may be a peer or someone in another department who can give you advice on business situations. Your coach may not even realize that he or she is a coach. Such colleagues are always good sources for business and industry advice. They know the people you work with and for.
- *Identify a sponsor.* Your sponsor should be someone at a higher level in your organization who will offer guidance. He or she should be in a position to influence your rise up the career ladder. The sponsor may be your direct superior or someone in a staff position.

Use your improvement staff as active resources. The wise guru can be asked questions you cannot take to coaches or sponsors. Coaches provide direct on-the-job guidance inside your company and in your customers' organizations. The sponsor helps you up the career ladder and provides protection when things go wrong.

I've noticed that field managers who are fountains of information about what is going on in an industry get their data from a few valued customers. Cultivate those supercoaches whose knowledge extends deep into your industry. They are valuable to you and can make you valuable to your senior contacts at headquarters.

BENCHMARK YOUR SALES PROCESS

A *benchmark* is a standard of reference by which something can be measured and judged. Business benchmarking is a methodology to use to compare your processes with those of others and shamelessly "steal" ideas to help you improve.

The objective is to uncover the best ideas in others' processes and then adopt those ideas in your own processes. The result is process superiority that leads to product and service superiority.

It takes a combination of smarts and humility to recognize that, whatever we do, someone, somewhere, has figured out a better, faster, cheaper, or easier way to do the same thing.

One company had a small share of the business in its industry. An internal team benchmarked every process related to the manufacture and distribution of the product. Ten years later, this company had a very large share of that business worldwide.

By benchmarking each step in the sales process, you find out where and how to improve. The *where* focuses efforts in the right place; the *how to* flows from studying how others perform the process step. Start "upstream" with benchmarking the prospecting process and end with the closing process.

Benchmarking begins with determining the process to benchmark and the partners from whom we want to learn. Next, we must make sure that we thoroughly understand our own process. Then we gather process data from both the public domain and benchmarking partners. Finally, information is analyzed and decisions are made concerning what can be implemented to improve our own processes.

Benchmarking sounds simple. However, it takes planning, time, and resources. As with everything else, an inadequate effort will bring inadequate results. When benchmarking is done correctly and thoroughly, a breakthrough in process improvement can be achieved.

Experience is a good teacher. However, it is other people's experience that is the best teacher. Don't let your own experience be your only teacher.

TIMELESS WISDOM

Seek other people's experience in books, tapes, and learning relationships. The objective is personal mastery of the sales profession, your customer's business, and your industry.

Part II

Planning
Wisdom

Any plan is only as good as your ability to change it. In war or selling, no plan survives the first contact in the field. Often the excuse for not having a plan is that plans are always changed. Plans cannot be rigid. Circumstances do change. We can't foretell the future, but we can plan for the futurity of decisions—that is, plan for a future in which we have the best options.

The purpose of the plan is to organize our thinking and get everything and everyone focused in the right direction. When an unforeseen obstacle gets in our way, we circumvent the obstacle. When someone moves the target, we adjust the plan.

Develop your plan by answering the simple questions What? Why? Who? How? Where? When?

Analyze your customer and his or her needs; then analyze your product or service. Meld the responses into your final sales plan:

- *What* do we want to accomplish? (Objective)
- *Why* should the customer buy from us? (Benefits)
- *Who* are key decision influencers? (Supporters and blockers)
- *How* do we present our case? (Methodology)
- *Where* will the buying decision be made? (Economic buyer or user buyer)
- *When* do we ask for the order? (Timing)

Every plan must be in writing. If a plan is not in writing, it is not a plan at all—it is only a dream or a vision but, perhaps more often, a nightmare.

After I left the corporate world, I regularly called my old customers when I visited their home city. In Oklahoma, my former customer was not at his place of business. I was given his home number. We met for lunch. Telling me that he had lost his business, he said, "I recall how many times you told me that I must have a plan in writing. I never had my plan in writing. I can't tell you how many times I've thought that if my plan had been in writing, I might still be in business!"

It's the process of putting things in writing that helps us think things through and organize for the future. Every written plan must have specific objectives and dates for accomplishing those objectives. Planning sales calls a week in advance and planning where and how we can get sales increases are examples of other planning standards.

Whatever goals you set (or have been assigned), the best planning strategy is to plan to exceed those goals every week and every month. Staying ahead of the sales plan keeps you in control and provides the opportunity for flexibility.

The wrong kind of pressure comes from trying to catch up on quota. With this type of pressure, the focus is on short-range objectives. Too often, this leads to "selling the order" instead of "building the business."

Here's a summary of planning components discussed in this book:

1. *Know their business.* Research starts with a document search for information about their company and industry. Read trade journals associated with the industry. Get copies of the company's annual and 10-K reports.

2. *Prepare your list of questions.* Develop a written list of questions that will uncover information vital to your success. Gather responses from the market.

3. *Know the key decision makers.* Learn about the personality of their president. For example, is he or she a reader or a listener? Is the decision-making style that of a "Lone Ranger" or of a team leader who discusses actions with the staff? Who are the key influencers?

4. *Be interactive.* Do not start conversations by saying what you can do. Find out what he or she needs. What is the

burning issue? Keep a dialogue going by probing with questions—too much talking and not enough listening loses sales.

5. *Stay focused.* Use visuals to reinforce key points in presentations or discussions. Keep the conversation on track.

6. *Identify results.* Discuss objectives. Talk about what can be achieved in terms of the organization's goals. Offer proof of your ability to deliver.

TIMELESS WISDOM

It's a fact. Successful people plan their work and work their plan. They know where they are going—and when they are going to arrive.

9
Get Your Strategy Right

A triumphant army
will not fight with the enemy until victory is assured.
An army destined to defeat will always fight with the opponent
first, in the hope that it may win by sheer good luck.
—Sun Tzu

 Simple paraphrases of this wisdom for sales strategies are

- A winning sales professional seeks his or her victories *before* engaging in the selling process.
- A salesperson destined to defeat sells in the *hope* of winning the sale.

Hope is not a method for winning sales; sound strategy is a method for winning sales.

THE ROLE OF STRATEGY AND TACTICS

Two key elements in every sales process are strategy and tactics. *Strategy* is an idea seeking its means of execution. *Tactics* are the means of execution used to carry out ideas.

45

Adm. Alfred T. Mahan, in *The Influence of Sea Power on History*, clearly explains how to differentiate strategy from tactics. He says, "Contact is a word which perhaps better than any other indicates the dividing line between strategy and tactics."

Strategy stops at the border in war. It stops at your office or car door in selling. Tactics begins with contact with the customer.

Strategy is doing the right thing. It is the planning component of the sales process. Strategy is war on paper. It is seeking victory before the battle.

Tactics is doing things right. It is the contact component of the sales process. It is the action of the war. It is the battle.

Planning the sales approach is strategic. Making the approach is tactical.

Planning whom to contact is strategic. Making the contact is tactical.

The business professional forms a strategy before the sale and executes tactics during the sales process. The strategy must be correct in order to succeed. There's no chicken-and-egg problem here. Strategy must always come first.

Successful offensive actions are launched when they are tactically feasible, even though another option may be strategically desirable. For example, strategically you may prefer to sell a specific product; however, tactically the customer may prefer a different product. Shifting the tactical action to take advantage of the circumstances does not alter the overall strategy.

The strategy must be right first; then the tactics can support the strategy. The converse is rarely true. Sustained tactical success—even continuous brilliant execution of tactics—seldom overcomes an inadequate strategic posture.

A bad strategy supported by good tactics can even be a fast route to failure; for example, tactical skill in selling large quantities of unprofitable products can be a fast route to bankruptcy.

STRENGTH AGAINST WEAKNESS

A basic principle of strategy is to concentrate strength against weakness. As applied to selling, this principle means that you must have the strength of enough benefits or added value to convince the prospect to purchase your product or service.

Sun Tzu's central proposition of "seeking victory before the battle" involves finding the critical selling points and benefits before beginning the sales process. This is good strategy.

The basics of good selling strategy are to plan a concentration of resources where

- Needs have been identified
- Competition is weak
- Profit potential is high

You must concentrate your resources where you can deliver results for the customer and earn a profit on the investment.

Priorities are important. The product or service performance has a higher priority than money. When you put profit first, you have the wrong strategy. Performance for the customer always precedes the financial decision. It's done successfully no other way.

KNOW WHEN TO STOP SELLING

As a senior manager, I can recall going out of my way to refer a new salesperson to another contact in my organization—even letting the contact know that the call was coming. Unfortunately, we already had another capable supplier for the service.

A few days later, the same salesperson called with a completely different service. Not only was I not interested in the new service, the salesperson lost his credibility by appearing to represent a wide range of services. I wondered, "What is his expertise?" I had never met him. How many services did he represent?

Did he care about any of them? If we develop a future need in areas he represents, he will not be on the list of people up for consideration.

TIMELESS WISDOM

Your strategic objective is to win the customer and nullify the opposition. Strategies that focus on the customer's needs while considering the opponent's weakness have the best odds for winning.

10
Win without Fighting

To subdue the enemy without fighting is the supreme excellence:

The best policy is to attack his strategy.
Second best is to disrupt his alliances
through diplomatic means.
Next best is to attack his army in the field.
The worst policy is to attack walled cities.

—Sun Tzu

Western strategic thought focuses on direct assaults and technological breakthroughs. Eastern strategic thought focuses on alliances and psychology. It follows that coalescing timeless wisdom from both Eastern and Western strategic thought puts you on the winning path. It's not that one approach is better than the other; you need the wisdom from both Eastern strategy and Western tactics. Know one, and you are only half prepared.

The key issue is to find ways to win the sale without direct confrontation with a competitor.

At the ultimate level is a loyal customer who prefers your products or services and returns repeatedly to buy from you.

"THE BEST SALES PRESENTATION IS THE ONE YOU NEVER HAVE TO MAKE."

I first heard that statement from my associate Tim Carpenter—a super sales professional. Carpenter explains, "When the customer calls because we've been recommended by a client, that's the best kind of selling situation. Then the meeting is not a presentation to get the business; it's a discussion to find out how we can best serve the customer."

A sales entrepreneur I know says that the Amway brand name helps him sell: "Sometimes the prospect is ready to sign up immediately upon learning that my servicing company is Amway Corporation. No detailed presentation is needed."

When the prospect approaches you because he or she has heard about you, the sale is half made. This happened when we received a call from a former client who was on the board of directors of another company. He wanted us to meet with the business principals. After several discussions, we began a major business engagement.

To achieve a reputation that attracts new business requires consistent superiority in performance. It's done no other way.

Our reputation either works for us or it works against us. The activities producing the reputation can be our most valuable asset because these processes keep existing customers and attract new ones.

GAIN VISIBILITY

You can help generate the visibility leading to a good reputation by being active in organizations, writing articles, and speaking at conferences. These public relations activities increase your exposure and help generate new contacts.

Speaking at programs gives you a wide audience. Don't try to sell your product or service during the presentation. Instead, be of service to the audience. Talk about ideas and information that members of the audience can use. It's OK to distribute your printed material. Instead of stacking it on a table, place it at every seat in the house. You can let the members of the audience qualify their interest for further information by providing cards they can fill out. If you can get a mailing list of the people in the audience, use it. If not, have them drop their business cards in a hat for a drawing. Follow-up is OK, but selling during your presentation turns off the audience. Don't do it. It's OK, however, to have the people in charge of the program mention your product or service.

Writing articles is another great visibility tool. Send copies of your article to the people on your private mailing list. Make copies of the next article and send it to everyone, and so on. The consistent flow trumpets your expertise as it reminds people that you are in business.

TESTIMONIALS ARE GREAT CREDENTIALS

The surest way to convince your prospect is with testimonials—the experiences of satisfied users. Happy customers can provide great credentials. They can say things you can't say.

The best testimonial is a person-to-person conversation between a prospect and a satisfied user. I've arranged for hundreds of contacts between prospects and star customers. Some have been by phone. However, the most successful have taken place when I escorted the potential buyer to the user's place of business. Then, I would find an excuse to leave them alone together at an appropriate time so my prospect could ask questions in private. The combination of serving as personal escort and allowing a private conversation often results in the sale. Nothing beats having the prospect ask a customer questions about his or her concerns and getting positive answers.

The next-best testimonials are letters or photographs. Letters from satisfied customers should be readily available to prospects.

An often-missed testimonial opportunity is a photograph of the product in use. For example, people who sell consumer durables can take pictures of *their* products in *their* customers' homes. Make a portfolio of photos showing the product in actual use: appliances in kitchens, furniture in rooms, or celebrities enjoying your products. Another good testimonial is a map with pins showing the location of customers.

MINIMIZE COMPETITIVE TALK

Note that the competitor's product was never mentioned during this process. The prospect may mention it, but you never, never do.

I learned this rule in a hardware store on Halstead Street in Chicago. I was employed as a field service manager by the Maytag Company, and my toolbox had been stolen. I went shopping for a new one. The clerk in one store turned to take a toolbox off the shelf, saying, "This one is every bit as good as a Kennedy." At that instant, I knew the brand name that was the standard of the industry and walked across the street to another store where I had seen a Kennedy toolbox. Note: Competitive parity comments such as "every bit as good as" do not make sales. When making a comparison, always point out the benefits of your unique features. For example, "The unique feature of this toolbox is its extra compartments that make it easy to organize small items and have them readily accessible."

Introducing a competitor's name in the conversation automatically telegraphs information to the prospective customer.

If the prospect asks, "Who is your competition?" providing a long list of people in your business is better than offering a short list of one or two names. Or, following with a question like, "Why would you consider anything (or anyone) else?" puts you back in control. If the prospect asks about a specific brand or competitor, ask for his or her opinion of that product or company.

If the prospect asks for a comparison with a competitor's product, do not make disparaging remarks. To recognize the question, offer a comment such as "They make an interesting product." If you have a point of competitive superiority, talk about it. Move on quickly to selling from the strength of your product. Talk about why you are outstanding in your field and why you are so differentiated that you really don't have any competition. Of course, the point of differentiation is only a feature, so you need to be sure to identify the benefit—what it will do for the customer.

Another effective way to talk positively about your product or service versus the competition's is to quote the endorsement of third parties such as a famous user or an article in a respected publication. Any kind of endorsement can move the attention back to the benefits from your product or service.

TIMELESS WISDOM

Follow the advice of Sun Tzu, who says the ultimate strategy is

- *To subdue the enemy's army without engaging it.*
- *To capture the enemy's cities without assaulting them.*
- *To overthrow his state without protracted operations.*

Perhaps, the ultimate sales strategy is

- To subdue the competitor without having to sell against him.
- To capture his customers without engaging in direct combat.
- To defeat the competition without spending a lot of time.

11
Know Your Competitor

If you know yourself, but not the enemy,
for every victory gained, you will suffer a defeat.
—Sun Tzu

 Sun Tzu further admonishes, "Know your enemy and know yourself, and in a hundred battles you will never be defeated." In a later time, the poet Ovid wrote, "It is right to learn, even from your enemy."

The sphere of knowledge that we must learn can be organized into three levels: product or service, people, and professional.

PRODUCT OR SERVICE KNOWLEDGE

The first level is thorough knowledge of competitive products or services—matched with complete knowledge of the industry. Of course, to make competitive knowledge useful, we must know our own product or service thoroughly so we can understand the differentiators. At trade shows, talk with suppliers, competitors, and their customers (the ones you sell and the ones you don't sell). Get to know more about their business than they do.

The editors of industry publications have a high level of knowledge about subjects that affect your business. Your advertising department probably places ads in industry publications and can put you in touch with the right people. Enlist the people in your advertising department and the agency as members of your intelligence team. Brief them on competitive brands and the types of information you seek.

PEOPLE KNOWLEDGE

The next level is knowledge of the competition on a personal level. Knowledge of the character and personality of individuals leads to understanding how they will act. From a study of their past employment history, you can predict how they will behave in the future. People tend to repeat what they learned in previous jobs. That's why companies like to hire people who had their early business training at organizations like Procter & Gamble and General Electric. We can identify this pattern of repetition of previously learned behavior from our own experience. For example, remember the new boss who came in and restructured the organization just the way it was at his former job?

Solicit feedback from your competitors' customers. This can be very useful in finding ways to penetrate these accounts.

PROFESSIONAL KNOWLEDGE

The next level of knowledge is of people who are not direct competitors but are engaged in similar processes. This would be anyone in the same profession or area of interest. Salespeople can learn from any other salesperson. Coaches and players in one sport can learn from coaches and players in another sport. This level of learning can be the source of creative ideas that achieve breakthroughs. If we knew what could be learned from others at this level, we wouldn't need to network with them—and that's the reason why we should network.

TIMELESS WISDOM

It's too easy to get trapped in a box—a box of normal contacts. Getting out of the box gets us out of our comfort zone. Out-of-the-box thinking exposes us to new opportunities.

12
Aim for Big Wins

Generally, management of a large force
is the same in principle as management of a few men;
it is a matter of organization.
—Sun Tzu

SELL THE BIG CUSTOMERS

It often takes no more time and effort to sell a large-volume account than a small one. What really counts is that the big customer can buy more than the small one.

Big companies not only buy big, they also gobble up a lot of other companies in mergers and acquisitions, so they have the potential of becoming even bigger customers.

Salespeople who call on some of the nation's largest accounts are occasionally asked to attend their customers' training sessions. For example, my friend who sells to WalMart and earned awards from WalMart has been invited to the company's Saturday morning meetings, where buyers exchange ideas. This inside information helps him be a better supplier.

Big accounts often serve as bell cows. They give us more credibility with other customers.

When helping a large consulting organization enter a new business, we targeted the big accounts in major markets. I found that the two largest accounts in major markets were already in business with our largest competitors. However, the third largest account was an excellent prospect. In the markets where the third largest account had recently made a management change in the department we were selling to, we had a very high potential prospect. Using this model of going to the third biggest account, we added big accounts in every major market.

TIMELESS WISDOM

If you aren't selling the big ones, keep on calling. The rewards can be worth it.

13
Learn from
Lost Sales

He who is not sage cannot use spies.
He who is not delicate and subtle
cannot get the truth out of them.
—Sun Tzu

We can't win every sale. One of the toughest things is rejection. When that happens, think about winning the next one.

If you sell every prospect, you are not making enough calls. If everything you try is a sure thing, you are not taking enough risks.

The key to success is being willing to fail and learning from failure. I've learned more from my sales failures than from my successes, especially when I've gone back and asked why I lost the sale. The only real loser is the person who doesn't get back up and fight again.

The story is told about the salesperson who said, "I made a big sale on Monday. I didn't sell anything on Tuesday. On Wednesday, the sale I made on Monday was canceled. Come to think of it, Tuesday was my best day."

My personal worst day is when I lose a sale, but one of my personal best days is when I find out why I lost a sale. The only thing that's worse than losing the sale is not knowing the real reason why you lost the sale.

The tendency is to offer excuses about why the customer didn't buy. Too often, much too often, I hear comments that place blame on the customer. When the customer doesn't buy, it's not because he's stupid; it's because we are stupid. We haven't established enough added value targeted at the customer's needs in our presentation.

Ninety-seven percent of customers are sold price, but only 3 percent buy price. It's a fact.

When hotel executives were asked to rank customer preferences in selecting a hotel, they listed price as the first reason. Presented with the same question, their customers ranked a good night's sleep at the top. How many times have you returned to a hotel where noise or a bad mattress kept you from getting a good night's sleep?

YOUR PERSONAL "LOST SALE" TRAINING

Treat each sales call as a potential learning experience. Whether you win or lose, ask yourself these questions:

"What did I do right?"

"What could I have done better?"

The most valuable training you will ever get is when the customer tells you the real reason why he or she did not buy. Getting that kind of honest information isn't easy. As Sun Tzu says, you need to be "delicate and subtle" to get the truth.

First, you must have established a good enough relationship with the prospect so that he or she is willing to tell you why you didn't make the sale. But you have to find a good way to phrase the question.

Your question could be a simple, "Just for my information, would you mind telling me what I (or we) did wrong?" Or

"What could we have done better?" Or, if you know that there have been several different presentations, "Just for my information, would you mind telling me about the other presentation that made you decide to buy?"

I like to open this kind of question with a comment like "just for my information" so the prospect knows that I'm not trying to argue. Whatever reason the prospect gives for making a decision, I express agreement with the decision. This helps get me get on the prospect's side so he or she doesn't hold back information. Gentle agreement is less reinforcing of a decision than disagreement, because disagreeing makes people want to justify their position. When the prospect responds with information, be sure to express appreciation for the valuable information.

USING WHAT YOU LEARN

On one occasion when I lost a sale and asked who had made the best presentation, I received an overview of a technique I've used in many presentations. Now I use the approach to make more sales. The concept involves opening a discussion with a question such as "What is the major problem you are facing?" In a group presentation, this open-ended question is asked of each individual in the room, and responses are listed on a flipchart. Now you know the problems people in this organization think they are facing. This means that your entire presentation can be focused on how your product or service can provide the best solution to their problems. It may be that the response reveals a lack of understanding of the real problems. If this is the case, direct your questions to surfacing issues important to them and you. Obviously, the concept works equally well in one-on-one situations.

On another occasion, the prospect who did not buy gave me the entire 30-page written proposal of my competitor. I thought the structure of the proposal was great, and I've incorporated the general outline into my proposals. Incidentally, when I visited the prospect to pick up the competitor's proposal, we talked about how we might deliver the next phase of services he would need.

Of course, even when you make the sale, it's a great idea to find out what your competitor did that the prospect liked—and, if you collect enough of that kind of information, you will win more sales. This data also enriches your knowledge of competitors and prepares you for the next offensive action.

TIMELESS WISDOM

Make the day you find out why the sale was lost your best day. There are some things your best friend won't tell you, but you can learn these things from prospects who did not buy from you—this time.

If you lose the sale, don't lose the prospect. He or she will be buying again from someone. Keep in touch. Find out how things are going. Send an article of interest, and then send another article.

Part III

Wisdom for Initiating Action

The fundamentals of establishing winning relationship were well stated in Dale Carnegie's *How to Win Friends and Influence People.* His guidelines apply today and are summarized here:

What you must do:
Begin in a friendly way.
Avoid arguments.
   Don't criticize, condemn or complain.
   Never tell the other person that he or she is wrong.
   If you are wrong, admit it.
Show respect for the other person's opinion.
Try to see things from the other person's point of view.
Be sympathetic with the other person's views and ideas.

What you must have the other person do:
Get him or her saying "Yes" immediately.
Let the other person do a great deal of the talking.
Let the other person believe that the idea is his or hers.

Arouse in the other person an eager want:
Appeal to the nobler motive.
Dramatize your ideas.
When nothing else works, throw down a challenge.

And to make the other people like you:
Be interested in them.
Make them feel important.
Smile, listen, and use their name.

FIND THE RIGHT
BEGINNING

Everything we do affects our opportunity to make the sale. Be yourself. Listen to the "beat" of the customer. Create a positive environment.

A customer's opinion is formed within the first few minutes of the meeting. Customers will find a way to buy from you if they like you and find a way not to buy from you if they do not like you.

Look for ways to build a relationship. Learning all you can about the customer's background before the meeting helps establish a common ground. It's great when you can start with comments such as, "Mr. Jones, I understand that you are president of the Widget Trade Association. Do you know Miss Smith?" (Of course, you know that he knows Miss Smith.)

If you can truly be sincere, make a comment of admiration about an item of personal dress. For example, "Where did you get that neat tie!" Find an item of interest in the surroundings, and ask about it. For example, "I really like this conference table."

When you begin a group presentation, a short, humorous comment can serve as an icebreaker. For example, when opening a workshop on quality management, I often begin with a question like "Will everyone in favor of quality please raise your hand?" This somewhat absurd question to an audience of quality managers earns a chuckle. The resulting laughter relaxes both the audience and me. It also gives me a lead-in to what I want to talk about: the fact that being in favor of quality isn't the problem; the problem is getting it implemented. Now I've got the audience focused.

In retail situations a customer should never be greeted with a question like "May I help you?" because the response could be "No." Instead, a more general question like "Isn't it a nice day?" or "How are you?" most often elicits a response that keeps the lines of communication open.

The challenge is that different circumstances require different behaviors. Finding the right beginning has much to do with arriving at a successful ending.

14
Seize the Initiative

He who occupies the field of battle first
and awaits his opponent is at ease.
—Sun Tzu

 The key to a successful offensive is skill, preparation, and above all, information. The norm is the confusion of not enough time, not enough resources, not enough skills training, and not enough information.

It would seem that the choice is often either to do it right later or to do it now. The successful sales professional must find that careful balance between getting ready and getting going. The greatest odds for success lie on the side of action. Most often, as soon as you do something, you become master of the situation.

LEAD GENERATION

In selling, the first step in launching the offensive is to search for prospects. The longer you wait, the greater the opportunity for your competitor to get there first. The "Rule of 45" says that 45 percent of all leads turn into a sale for someone. Too many people stop following up on leads. For that reason, old leads might have less competition.

The missionary work required to introduce a new product or service can be difficult and time consuming. However, when you are first with a highly differentiated product, no one steals your prospective customers with a lower price.

The best way to begin building a sales relationship is to sell something—that "something" could be a minor product or service. This minor sale is a *door opener* that gives you a reason to keep coming back.

Getting started is what's important. After getting started, concentrate on growing from the base.

COLD CALLS

Diving into cold call selling is like diving into a cold pool. Thinking about getting in is worse than being there. So when you get started, keep right on cold calling. It's better than getting out of the water and having to think about getting back in again.

You can't do good cold call selling in a nonsupportive atmosphere. That's why companies who do most of their business via cold call selling have regular pep meetings.

Set up your own pep atmosphere. Think about when you've been most comfortable and successful making cold calls. Replicate the situation.

MAKING COLD CALLS WARM

If you can find a thread of commonality, the cold call isn't really a cold call at all. Asking your customers for the names of prospects automatically gives you a name to use as a link and an implied endorsement. Sending a letter gives you an opening; for example, "Last week, I sent you a letter on . . . ." If you are getting prospects' names out of newspapers or magazines, sending them a mounted reprint can help make your call more welcome.

When a prospect suggested that I send a brochure before she agreed to an appointment, I sent the brochure. When I called back, she didn't remember getting the brochure or my previous call. So

I sent the brochure in a box containing a chocolate chip cookie the size of a giant pizza with a note saying, "Here's the cookie with the message." When I called back, she said, "You made my day. When do you want to come in?" I made the call, got the order, and began a long relationship with a new customer.

Although you may not know the individual, you can, and must, do research on the company.

When the prospect asks for a brochure during a phone call, he or she is often trying to end the conversation. Use the request as an opportunity to probe by saying, "Yes, I'll be happy to do that. I'll need to ask just a few questions to make sure that I send the appropriate brochure."

MAKING THE FIRST CALL

If the first call is by phone, keep it short. Keep your objective in mind—your objective is (probably) to get an appointment.

When making the first call, be prepared. Know the customer and his or her business and be able to explain your product or service briefly. This brief summary is often called an *elevator speech*. The descriptive term identifies the short time available for your monologue. For example, you get on an elevator on the first floor and encounter a great prospect. She asks, "What will your product do for me?" You must respond with a sales-oriented answer before she gets off on the tenth floor.

More often than you would like, your first (and last?) introduction will be via telephone. The "What's in it for the customer?" needs to come out fast in the conversation. The person receiving a cold call is rapidly processing the following types of questions:

- Is there anything in this for my company?
- If there is, can I reasonably get to it?
- How much effort will it take to get to the brass ring being offered?
- Do we have the infrastructure to support this?

69

- Does it fit with our strategy?
- Could we make room in our budget?
- Am I the right contact?
- Does the person presenting this opportunity have enough credibility that I should even consider moving forward on this?
- Does this person present him- or herself well?
- Does this person seem to understand my company and our position?
- Was this person referred to me by someone I trust?

Be sure to do your research—know about the prospect, and the prospect will want to know about you. Don't be in the position of the salesperson who had to give a negative answer to this question, posed by a retail chain executive: "Have you been in any of our stores?"

When the first call is in person, have a standard list of questions ready. Direct the conversation so that you can elicit information about the prospect and others. You want to know everything from the organization's major problems to the buyer's vacation habits. The list of questions could be very long, and you may need to make several calls to complete the list. Facts like the buyer's vacation preferences may come from a secretary or receptionist—or from other suppliers. This broad base of information is a component of a good relationship. When you know where a customer likes to go on vacation, you have a clue to a unique Christmas gift.

TIMELESS WISDOM

An old adage says, "You've got to get there firstest with the mostest." If you get there first, you've automatically got the "mostest." If you can't get there first, then work on having the "mostest."

15
Feed the Funnel

The possibility of victory lies in the attack.
—Sun Tzu

 The first line of attack in sales is lead generation. Consider the lead generation process to be separate from the selling process. When we combine lead generation with the selling process, we tend to spend too much time with regular customers and not enough time developing new prospects.

There are many levels of lead generation activity, ranging from direct mail, to networking, to personal prospecting calls.

I've heard talk about the sales pipeline as if there were such a thing. There is no pipeline that converts a prospect into a customer. All lead generation is funnel work; that is, it takes a large number of contacts to eventually make a sale. A lot of activity has to take place at the top of the funnel in order to get results at the bottom.

The ten-eight-four-two-one funnel is an example of the sales results that can be achieved in prospecting a popular product:

- Initiate contacts to *ten* people.
- *Eight* will be available (that is, in the office or at home).
- *Four* can be engaged in a conversation.
- *Two* will be interested in your product or service.
- *One* will result in a sale.

In this example, it is easy to see that you must initiate more contacts to make more sales. The same principle applies in every sales channel. In one industry, for example, it takes 125 contacts to get 5 solid prospects, and only 1 of the prospects will result in a sale.

To make the lead generation process work, focus on getting prospects into the funnel—the input. Too often, people want to focus on the results. Nothing can be squeezed out of an empty funnel. Little comes out if little is put in. It takes a lot of work at the top of the funnel to get results. Plan your network at the top of the funnel, and your plan will work at the bottom. After the process is working, try to increase the effectiveness of the process.

The amount of precious metal that a refiner gets from ore depends on two factors—quantity and quality. The number of sales you make depends on the number and the kind of people you see. Go for quantity (numbers) in areas where there is high quality (people with buying potential).

Participate in a lead-sharing group. This activity will keep you focused on generating new business.

NETWORKING

The objective of building a network is to create relationships that lead to sales. People want to do business with people they know, like, and trust.

Here are some rules for cultivating a successful network:

- Go to trade shows, association meetings, and business events with the objective of meeting the difference makers—the officers and editors who are at the center of influence.
- Talk about their business and their interests. Not yours.
- Focus on helping them be more successful. Networking can be a trading process. Help them, and they will help you.

- Get their business cards, and send handwritten notes telling them you will try to send business to them (or be of service).
- Follow up with articles of interest to them.
- Find ways to keep in contact; Send more articles, send leads, send thank-you notes when you get any communication from them. (Emails are OK, but short handwritten notes are better, much better.) Call someone you have not talked to in a while.

A good way to make the funnel work is to draw a funnel. Then list the sources that feed the funnel. The sources could be activities like speeches at meetings and conferences, phone canvassing, advertising leads, referrals, and personal networking. To test how well these lead sources are working, check the date of the most recent new name you've acquired in each group. If the most recent date of acquisition in any group is old, that channel probably needs some stimulation.

Then separate the funnel into several sections:

- *Lead universe.* These are names you want to get into the funnel. They have potential interest in your product or service.
- *New suspects.* These are the leads in the funnel who meet some of your qualifications for a prospect.
- *Current prospects.* These are former suspects who you know can benefit from your product or service. They are on your current contact list.

Names that go through the funnel should be recycled:

- *Active accounts.* These are current customers who will make additional purchases.
- *Previous accounts.* These are old customers who could move back into active status.

Segmenting the funnel is a method for keeping the funnel active.

KEEP ACTIVE

Don't get trapped into waiting for prospects to buy. Keep filling the funnel. Brainstorm a list of all the people who could benefit from your product or service. Reward customers who provide references. Look for new ways to find new leads and keep mining the mine. Have a goal for the number of different kinds of contact activities you will make each month. Think about people you can know today who will be good prospects tomorrow.

TIMELESS WISDOM

Keep filling the funnel. The funnel works when we make it work.

16
Sell from Strength

An army superior in strength
takes action like the bursting of pent-up waters
into a chasm of a thousand feet deep.
—Sun Tzu

 Don't concentrate on worrying about your weaknesses. Instead, focus on the strengths of who you are and what you can do. Build your world and your customer's world around the strengths of your product, your service, and yourself.

MINIMIZE WEAKNESS

Unfortunately, the natural tendency is to reinforce weakness. When we lose a sale, we can become obsessed with the weakness we think caused the loss. Focusing thinking on real or imagined weakness can be a self-fulfilling prophecy. All products, services, and people have some weakness. It's important to know both our own weaknesses and those of our competitors, but don't dwell on the weakness of your product or service or on some aspect of your personal weakness.

Because smart competitors will attack your weakness, you need to be alert to the threat. However, when on the offensive (always be on the offensive), sell from strength. Note: Being "on the offensive," does not mean "being offensive."

REINFORCE STRENGTH

We can be more productive by focusing on our strengths because focusing on reinforcing weaknesses requires a lot of time and reinforced weaknesses are often not great competitive strengths. Focusing on strengths is focusing on what we do best.

Selling from strength requires that we do our homework. Product and service strengths are relative to what the customer wants and what the competition has to offer. Too often, we think of our strengths only in terms of what we have to offer. That's the wrong focus. Customers don't care about what we have to offer unless it's what they want.

If customers are getting what they want from a competitor, we need enough strength to dislodge that competitor. Being as good as the competitor isn't good enough to dislodge a competitor. Our product or service must be perceived as being better, often considerably better, in order to replace that competitor.

Reinforcing strength is the principle used in the German blitzkrieg during World War II. That is, launch a massive assault on a wide front to search for places where penetration can be made. As the German troops moved into a country, they attempted to go around the opposition instead of fighting the resistance. Each time they met opposition, they went around it.

The same principle applies in the sales blitz. Temporarily go around opposition and penetrate where you can. Here's a process for blitzing a sales effort:

- Think about selling your product or service to a type of customer or in a specific geographic area.
- Brainstorm a list of potential customers in that sector.
- Initiate a large number of contacts in a limited period of time.

- When you encounter opposition, try another approach or go on to the next prospect. (Come back later with a different approach.)

Salespeople who are selling new products or venturing into new territories will find the concept of the blitzkrieg particularly beneficial.

TIMELESS WISDOM

The blitzkrieg concept is simply calling on a large number of prospects in a concentrated period of time and selling where there is the least resistance. After the first pass, go back to mop up the resistance.

17
Teamwork Works

When the troops are united,
the brave cannot advance alone, nor can the cowardly retreat.
—Sun Tzu

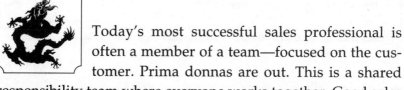 Today's most successful sales professional is often a member of a team—focused on the customer. Prima donnas are out. This is a shared responsibility team where everyone works together. Good sales teams don't just happen. It takes time, team training, and shared experiences to build a team.

People working together can achieve much more than any single individual. Successful teamwork is not a goal; it is a living organization that melds, grows, and gains strength.

In an ever-increasing number of selling situations, the sales professional facilitates the relationship between people at many levels in his or her company with people at many levels in the customer's company in order to maximize a mutually productive relationship.

When most people think of business teams, they think of meetings. Certainly, meetings are a part of teamwork, but sales teams are more virtual because members are often not at the same location. Sales teams represent a coordination of various organizational functions and interactions with the prospect and his or her team. How to hold effective team meetings is well documented in many fine books. We'll focus here on other aspects of teamwork.

Gen. Robert Neyland retired in 1952 from coaching football at the University of Tennessee with a record of 173-31-12. Teamwork was his first priority as revealed in a few of his football maxims:

- A team that won't be beat can't be beat.
- Eleven men in every play.
- Play your own position well first.

Tony DiCicco served as head coach of the U.S. Women's National Soccer Team that won an Olympic Gold Medal; in 1999 he coached the World Cup Championship team. To build team unity, he used mental exercises. Shortly before the Cup competition began, each player was given an "imaging" tape, a short video of her skills choreographed to music of her choice. During the final week, inspirational quotes were slipped under the players' doors every day. Roommates were switched regularly to prevent cliques from forming.

Author Mariah Burton Nelson tells about what team sport athletes know:

- *They know who their teammates really are.* Teammates who don't just sympathize, but help us achieve success.
- *They know how to compete.* Nonathletes tend to believe friends should not compete. Athletes do not see competition as divisive; they use it to connect.
- *They know how to bond.* Team athletes have a shared vision and support one another.
- *They know how to take risks.* They are willing to take risks such as passing the ball to someone else in soccer.
- *They know how to ask for help.* We really don't have to be perfect.

- *They know how to forgive themselves.* They stop apologizing and focus on their next achievement.

Management consultant T. Allen Pannell, Jr., who has worked with many winning sales teams, lists the following teamwork attributes for sales professionals:

- *Common purpose.* The effective sales professional will help clarify and create common purpose among team members. The mission should be defined and communicated. However, the unique needs of each team member must be understood to avoid conflicts and create win-win solutions.
- *Roles and responsibilities.* When you find someone "messing in your piece of the pie," this is usually a sign of unclear roles. The selling side of the team must be absolutely clear on one another's roles. Any confusion in this area is unprofessional and can easily cost sales. A quick sit-down (or stand-up) meeting to brainstorm all the roles in a given sales process and verify assigned responsibilities will usually handle most of the issues. Turf wars must be solved immediately or mediated by higher management, if necessary.
- *Procedures.* Tasks must be defined. How will communication occur, decisions be made, and information be documented? How will meeting dates and times be set? How will meetings be run and conflict handled? Even though there are many proven answers to these questions, it is most important they be asked and addressed. The method selected is secondary to a mutual understanding of how tasks will be defined.
- *Trust.* Trust comes from always keeping one's word. Trust can't be rushed; trust takes time to develop. Management's responsibility is to ensure that the systems and practices in place promote trust. If the reward system creates competing interests among the sales team, trust will be an issue.

- *Synergy.* People who have participated in some sort of problem-solving exercise as team. members know the power of team solutions. These exercises vividly demonstrate the synergistic power of teams. The team answer to a problem is often better than any individual's answer or the average answer of the team members working alone. Synergy demonstrates that the whole is greater than the sum of the parts.

To achieve synergy, that is, to create results beyond what could be accomplished individually, a team needs the following hallmarks:

- Open communication
- Full participation (not necessarily equal participation)
- Commitment to team decisions
- Shared leadership—everyone is responsible for the success of the team, not just the leader
- Process checks—routine straight talk about how the team is doing

---

TIMELESS WISDOM

Teams do better. Teams accomplish more. Don't sell solo when you can have the strength of the team.

18
Time and Timing
Aid Victory

*While we have heard of stupid haste in war,
we have not yet seen a clever victory that was prolonged.*
—Sun Tzu

Time is your greatest ally and your greatest enemy. Budgeting time is as important as budgeting finances. Here are the key issues of time in selling:

- *As a rule, earliest is best.* Decision time saved is selling time gained.
- *One can feel protected from falling only when one is rising.* Successful sales campaigns require continual action. It's called momentum.
- *If you wait for approval from headquarters, you will be too late.* When you ask for approval, there will be a delay in response, and competitors will have had time to act.
- *Do not delay a decision because of incomplete information.* You never have all the information you need.
- *Rapid decision making produces rapid action.* The shorter the decision time, the sooner the action can be implemented, and the greater the probability you will outmaneuver a competitor.

- *Rapid action is simultaneous action.* When speed is at a maximum, processes that need to be focused on a point in time are simultaneous.
- *Delayed decisions inevitably lose their positive quality.* When you wait too long, your enemies have had time to prepare, and your friends have lost patience.
- *All the positive consequences of speed accrue to the early offensive.* The less you delay your offensive, the less apt you are to be surprised and the less ready your competitor will be. Also, the less you delay your offensive, the greater the probability your time of attack will be earlier than expected by your competitor, who will then be surprised by all the consequences that follow.

TIMELESS WISDOM

Everything works right at the right time. Speed builds its own momentum.

19
Be a Gorilla— or Be a Guerrilla

Use many to strike the few.
—Sun Tzu

The big corporate gorilla fights with overwhelming strength—anywhere it wants to fight.

The small business guerrilla also fights with overwhelming strength—but only at a time and place of his or her own choosing.

Each can win. Each can lose. Each commands a relative superiority at the time of battle.

One of the major principles in the rise of the Red Chinese Army was that territory has no relevance. Chairman Mao said, "When the enemy advances we retreat. When the enemy retreats we advance." Guerrillas survive by protecting the territory where they are located. It does not matter what territory they hold. The key is survival. Guerrillas win by being where the "gorilla" isn't.

The first guerrilla was a French commando leader. In his time, he reduced English possessions in France to a thin strip without fighting a single major battle. He avoided the major concentrations of the enemy and "nibbled." When something went wrong, he called off the attack.

Every business entrepreneur is a guerrilla who finds territory that can be held. Sales representatives strengthen their organizations by adding strong lines and dropping weak ones. When a rep has major product lines, he or she can occasionally act like a gorilla. Most often the rep's strategy is that of a guerrilla who looks for opportunities where temporary superiority can be achieved.

Here are rules for sales guerrillas as adapted from Lawrence of Arabia:

- Do not go head to head against gorillas. Go where gorillas do not go and do things that gorillas do not do.
- Attack when and where your opponent is weak.
- Watch for screwups and move rapidly. Sometimes, the way to win is to capitalize on mistakes.
- Don't attack with your weakness. Lead from strength. When your strengths are very strong, your weaknesses are not as vulnerable.
- You may have limited resources; however, knowledge of what is going on is never limited. Personal reconnaissance should be a high priority.
- Employ psychological warfare. It's good psychology to appear bigger and stronger—being highly professional is just one of the ways to do this.
- Small forces emphasize speed and time. For example, focus on prompt, dependable service—this is your value added. Keep your customer informed when service will be late.

TIMELESS WISDOM

Guerrillas select a time and place where they can have overwhelming strength. Gorillas sleep wherever they want.

20
Take Calculated Risks

To assemble the host of his army and bring it into danger—
this may be termed the business of the general.
—Sun Tzu

 Hockey great Wayne Gretsky says, "I missed every shot I didn't take."

It's the same in selling: We lose 100 percent of the sales for which we do not ask. Of course, asking isn't without problems. Requests for the order that are too transparent do not work.

All of life is risk taking. In many situations, not doing something can be a bigger risk than taking action. It was said of Gen. George McClellan, at the Battle of Antietam during the Civil War: "He was so fearful of losing, he could not win."

In any negotiation, the side that is willing to lose can win. The side that cannot afford to lose will find negotiating difficult, especially if the other side becomes aware of its need to win. Thousands of years ago, the Chinese strategist Wu Chi wrote, "The battlefield is a land of standing corpses. Only those who are willing to die can live." The same lesson applies to business engagements: Those who are willing to risk losing have an advantage.

Those who walk away from the negotiating situation never know the minimum the other side is willing to accept. In the bazaars of the world, the best negotiators get the best price when they start to walk away. That's when the trader knows that he is about to lose the opportunity to make the sale and quickly offers a lower price.

Bill Richardson, governor of New Mexico and former ambassador to the United Nations, gives his negotiating rules:

1. Make friends.
2. Define your goal.
3. Shrug off insults.
4. Always show respect.
5. Close the deal.

Richardson says, "Cede the easy territory." In his case, he often ceded the easy territory by going to a foreign country to negotiate. To win your goals and close the deal, be sure to point out what is in the interest of the other side.

The only real loser in negotiations is the person who doesn't get back up after falling down.

TIMELESS WISDOM

Although you should mentally and physically exert every effort to make the sale, don't be overwhelmed with concern about losing. Instead, focus on creating the quietly confident atmosphere that makes the other side fear that he or she might lose something by not doing business with you.

21
When Things Go Wrong

Five musical notes yield more melodies
than can ever be heard.
Five basic pigments produce more colors
than can ever be seen.
Five cardinal tastes yield more flavors
than can ever be tasted.
Two postures in battle
combine to an endless series of maneuvers.
—Sun Tzu

 Uncontrollable variations can cause things to go wrong. The resulting problems provide opportunities to be a hero to the customer.

INITIATE ACTION

When the customer has a problem, leap into action. Whether or not you solve the problem, it is important to be available to listen to the customer talk about the problem. Show empathy and take action.

A study by Abt Associates of Cambridge, Massachusetts, showed a direct correlation between customer dissatisfaction and the number of people the customer had to talk to before the problem was resolved.

The time it takes to solve a problem is another important element. The same study showed that customers who received answers within 10 days were much more likely to be satisfied with the response, regardless of the response, than customers who had to wait longer. It's the "if only they would give me an answer" syndrome.

GO BEYOND SOLUTIONS

A friend staying at the Oriental Hotel in Tokyo was sent a fax by an associate in another country who called to tell him the fax was on the way. After waiting for a while, my friend called the front desk. The fax was finally delivered. Later, he reported his dissatisfaction to the assistant manager, who apologized and insisted on doing something extra to make amends. This type of something extra is called a *value-added atonement*. It's a good way to reduce the risk of losing a customer.

When the customer isn't happy, saying you are sorry is not enough. When we waited a long time for service at a restaurant, the chef came to our table to apologize and tell us why the service was slow. Nice, but we were not really interested in his problems; we wanted our dinner in a reasonable amount of time. Beware of an explanation that attempts to make your problem the customer's problem. An explanation is fine as long as it ends with an acceptable solution or valued-added atonement to the customer. By the way, we didn't return to the restaurant. Now we can't go back because it is closed.

At another restaurant where we had slow service and complained, the manager said management knew it had a problem and the problem would be corrected. He asked us to return for a free dinner. We've returned many times. The parking lot is always full.

Although customer service may not be your area of responsibility, the level of customer service has a direct effect on your ability to get repeat business. Check it out.

HAVE A PROCESS FOR FIXING PROBLEMS

Here is a simple formula for handling problems when things go wrong:

1. Respond immediately.
2. Apologize. Let the customer know that you regret the problem.
3. Ask what the customer wants you to do to correct the situation. (Often, the customer will ask for less than you expect.)
4. Take action.
5. Offer a value-added atonement.

TIMELESS WISDOM

Customers don't care how much you know until they know how much you care.

Part IV

Wisdom for Structuring the Sale

First: *Create a Need*
Second: *Maximize the Need*
Third: *Fill the Need*
        and
        Follow Up

 The best sales structures are simple frameworks built around the basics of good business communication.

- Create a Need

  Establish a relationship. Look for anything that establishes a sense of relationship or personal credibility. People buy from friends, and you want to be a friend.

  Find a need. Identify needs by asking questions and listening to the answers. Beware of the tendency to talk about what you have to sell. Find out the customer's needs.

- Maximize the Need

  Verify the need. Sift through the discussion to find the reality. The more clearly you establish the need, the greater the opportunity of winning the sale. Have customers confirm that "this is what they want."

  Scope up the need. Amplify the need to the maximum while reducing costs to the ridiculous.

- Fill the Need

  Find solutions. This is a mutual discovery exercise. Responses from previous questions will help you lead the discussion. Beware of rote presentations. Keep in mind what you know about personality preferences. Use logic with a thinker, and appeal to the emotions of a feeler. Use visuals.

  Handle objections. Keep in mind that objections are simply requests for more information. You want the prospect to talk so you can get objections out in the open.

  Ask for the order. It takes practice to learn how to read buying signals. The simple rule for asking for the order is "too soon and too often." This is a subtle request. Ask too little and too late and you will never get a sense of timing.

- Follow Up

  Keep in touch. You do not want to just make sales; you want to build customers. It's the repeat business and referrals that make you successful.

KEEP IT SIMPLE

The more complex your offer and presentation, the less liable it is to be understood and acted upon.

During President Bill Clinton's winning campaign, the managers kept their focus on a single simple issue by posting a sign on the wall at headquarters that read, "It's the economy, stupid." This was an effective use of the KISS principle—Keep It Simple, Stupid.

Most presentations are improved by taking something out, not by adding more. The more you say, the less gets through.

Never give more than three reasons for buying your product or service. The longer your list, the less likely it is to be remembered.

Never list more than three topics on a visual at one time. If you really need a longer list, break it into subheadings, and use three smaller points under each.

If your prospects need to pass information to someone else in their organization, give them only three things to remember, such as the three reasons for buying from you.

HAVE BOTH FORM AND SUBSTANCE

Don't get so hung up on the substance of your presentation that you forget about form. Form is not just the physical appearance of a proposal; it's every little thing you do that reinforces your personal and corporate credentials and professionalism.

LITTLE THINGS MEAN A LOT

Selling is like banking: You have to make deposits before you can make withdrawals. Paying attention to the following little things can add up to big sales:

- Tell the truth. If you can't tell the truth, selling is the wrong profession for you. Please find something else to do.
- Know your customer's birthday, anniversary, family names, and hobbies.
- Have an adequate supply of business cards. Keep a backup supply in your luggage or glove compartment.
- Give business leads to friends. They will return the favor.
- When you see poor quality in your company, speak up pleasantly and firmly about the need for improvement. Silence is acceptance.
- Underpromise and overperform. Keep cool. Never respond in anger. Follow David Ogilvy's advice: "Never send a letter on the day you write it."
- Say the magic words "Please," "Thank you," and "I appreciate you." This is as good an idea at home and in the office as it is with your customer.
- Use the customer's name frequently in every conversation.
- Keep your car clean—inside and outside.
- Make your boss look good—so that he or she can get promoted.
- Train a replacement—so that you can get promoted.
- When the customer says "Yes," that's no little thing. That's the time to leave. Stay too long, and you'll leave without the order.

The First Step:
CREATE A NEED

It's easy to get into a discussion about whether sales professionals are need fillers or want creators.

The story is told about the man who had to move to an apartment in the big city. Circumstances did not allow him to take along his fine Collie dog. He offered the dog to a farmer who turned him down, saying that he did not want a dog of any kind. The man related the turndown experience to a friend.

The friend, who was a sales professional, went to visit the farmer. He told the farmer that he often drove by the farm and was so impressed by its appearance that he wanted to meet the owner.

The farmer offered to show him around and pointed with pride to his buildings. The friend asked the farmer whether he had problems with rats. The farmer said that he did not know what to do about the rats. When the friend saw the herd of cattle, he asked the farmer whether he had problems getting them into the barn at night. The farmer acknowledged that he was getting on in years and could use some help. When they walked around the open fields, the friend asked the farmer whether he was concerned about robbers. The farmer told about a theft that had occurred at a nearby house. Our friend discussed how a prosperous farmer could be at even greater risk than a homeowner.

The friend said, "If you had a really good farm dog, he probably would give you a sense of security, help round up the cows, and kill the rats, wouldn't he?" "Yes," said the farmer. "I've often thought that what I need is a good farm dog. If you could find a good one, I'd pay as much as $100 for the right one." The friend replied, "I think I know about just the right dog for you."

That's right. The farmer paid $100 for a dog he could have had at no charge. Note that our sales professional used questions to create the need. Then he asked more questions. The farmer provided the theft information to help maximize the need. Only when the farmer confirmed the definite need for a dog did the friend offer to fill the need. This is just one example of how to create, maximize, and fill a need.

Consultants have a saying: "Find out what they want, and sell them what they need." First, it is necessary to ask questions to uncover a customer's wants. Sometimes what customers think they want is not the best solution to fill their needs. The best service you can render is to uncover the real need and fill it.

Organize your sales discussion so that the powerful benefit of your product or service creates the need.

22
Set the Stage

When crossing mountains,
be sure to stay in the neighborhood of valleys.
When encamping,
select high ground facing the sunny side.
When high ground is occupied,
do not ascend to attack.

—Sun Tzu

 Like Sun Tzu's advice about crossing mountains, encamping, and fighting up hill, a few simple rules can help set the stage for your meeting with the customer. Careful planning ensures that the dialogue takes place in the most favorable circumstances.

PREPARING TO GO ON STAGE

It's fundamental: Good preparation yields good results. Knowledge is vital.

We have only one chance to make a good first impression. New customers form an impression of us very early in the first meeting.

During inclement weather, get rid of your outer coat before meeting the contact; don't look like someone who just came in off the street. Find a place to hang your coat; lay it on a chair or throw it in a corner. Do not burden the customer with hanging up your coat.

Dress like your customer. If you aren't sure what the customer will be wearing, it's better to be dressed more conservatively than your prospect. If you are more casual than your contact, it might be seen as disrespectful. In the United States, the farther west you go, the greater the tendency to dress casually for business. In Europe, dress, as well as salutations, is much more formal.

THE STAGE SETTING

When entering an office, select nonconfrontational seating arrangements. Persuasion is easier when you are seated alongside someone rather than across a solid barrier like a desk or table.

When several people on the same selling team are going to be in a conference room, the team members should arrive ahead of the customer. Select seats interspersed around the table so that you will be alongside the people you are trying to persuade. Do not bunch up on one side of the table so that it's "them" versus "us."

THE PERFORMANCE

Match your eye level to the customer's eye level. If the customer is standing, you should be standing. If the customer is seated, you should be seated.

The mind is faster than the mouth. We speak at a rate of about 125 words a minute; our minds think at a rate of 500 words a minute. That disparity gives the mind ample opportunity to wander. Do things to keep the interest level high. Interact with the participants, and use high drama when appropriate. Put on a memorable show.

Make it a habit to address the customer frequently by name. That's what friends do. Being addressed by name generates a wealth of good feelings because

- Using the name shows personal interest.
- Using the name indicates special attention.
- Using the name creates a personal linkage.
- Using the name impresses the customer.

Make your presentation visually interesting. I attended a seminar in which the message was that every visual could be an illustration. What an interesting way to deliver a memorable message!

Advertisers say that the maximum number of words for any billboard is fourteen—keep the word count down on each visual. Use no more than three major points on a visual. If you have to apologize because some members of the audience can't read the visual, do not use the visual. Color adds vitality. Use it to high-light key points.

Visuals that dominate the presentation can distract from the message. Avoid the tendency to do too many cute things with PowerPoint presentations.

Not all your visuals need to be on the screen. Here are ideas that add visual interest to any presentation:

- *Magnify.* Big props carry the message better than small props do. For example, a 6-foot teddy bear is more dramatic than a 6-inch one.
- *Involve.* Get customers involved in the demonstration. Let them touch, taste, visit, or drive what you are selling.
- *Envision.* What is the customer's dream? Paint a picture of a great future. Use possessive words such as "your" and optimistic words such as "can be."
- *Give examples.* Show how well the product works. Have an actual sample—in miniature, if necessary.

- *Illustrate.* A pie chart or bar graph is a better visual illustration than a list of numbers.

Although it may be necessary to stand while using visuals in front of a seated group, sit down when it is comfortable to do so. This can be particularly important when engaging in a dialogue. It's always better to be at the same eye level with another person when trying to reach agreement. Seated people have a natural resistance to persuasion from those who are standing because the standing position tends to be dominating.

Professionals clean up when they leave. If you accepted a cup of coffee, then disposing of the empty cup is your responsibility. Don't leave anything behind that needs to be cleaned up.

The selling stage is ours to set. Leave nothing to chance. Let the competitor do that. Heed these simple rules for effective presentations:

- *Do not have a written script.* You will read it word for word, and that is bad.
- *Do not use extensive notes.* You will become a slave to the words in the notes.
- *Involve the audience.* Ask questions; solicit feedback.
- *Use visuals.* They help get your message across and increase retention.
- *Do your homework.* Be knowledgeable about the participants' backgrounds and interests.
- *Practice, practice, practice.*

THE PHONE IS A VERBAL STAGE

Answering machines and voice mail are wonderful conveniences that can be barriers to anyone in sales. Avoid leaving a message on an answering machine (or even with a message taker) asking someone who doesn't know you to call back.

Why would someone who is besieged with calls return a stranger's call? And what if the prospect calls back and gets your answering machine or voice mail? Even worse, what if the prospect calls back and you can't recall the person's name or why you left the message in the first place. This can be embarrassing to you and irritating to the caller.

Every study I've ever seen indicates that abdicating your presence to voice mail actually diminishes your chances of making the sale.

What's the best thing to do when you find yourself in that nether world of voice mail? You have several options: The best choice can be to contact an assistant to find out the best time to call back. If the assistant doesn't know or is being uncooperative, ease yourself out of the conversation and call back another time. Sometimes, it's possible to get through to your contact by calling early, late, or during the lunch hour when the assistant is often gone.

In most situations, don't ask to be called back. If anything, refuse the offer to get you to leave a message by telling the message taker that you are going to be out of the office and difficult to reach. Why? Because the minute you ask a prospect to return your call, you lose the initiative.

There is an exception to this rule: If you have developed some level of relationship with the person you are trying to call, you might choose to leave your name and phone number. Leaving the name of the person who suggested that you call is often effective.

The messages to your incoming callers are also important. Instruct your assistant to use the "out to lunch" phrase only during normal lunch hours. If you are reported as out to lunch at 2 PM, your caller may get the wrong idea.

Telephones are great communication devices when you structure the circumstances so that the telephone can be used to your advantage.

YOUR EMAIL IS YOU!

Email is a fast way to communicate. It's easy to make careless mistakes with email, so be careful.

One study shows that words in verbal communication are only 7 percent of the message, tonal inflection is 38 percent of the message, and nonvocals such as facial, eye, and body movements are 55 percent of the message content. Obviously, much of the "feel" of the communication is lost in written communication.

Consider these guideposts:

- The written word can appear more critical than the spoken word. Sensitive personal information and comments that might be taken as criticism should always be delivered in person—no exceptions!
- Never communicate bad news via email. You can't communicate feelings effectively by email, and you can't read the other person's reactions.
- A written sell of an idea can be a one-way carrier pigeon taken as an edict—and mentally rejected. You need interactive communication to get your sell received by the other person.
- Thank-you emails are convenient, but a thank-you note is more personal.

Email does have good uses in communication:

- It's great for follow-ups and updates. Short emails can demonstrate good follow-through or a sense of urgency.
- Keeping in touch by email keeps you uppermost in the customer's mind while showing respect for the customer's time.

It's often wise to let time pass (at least a few hours) between writing a communication and sending it. Then, proof your communication for grammar and context. You'll often be glad you did. Written communication is always improved by taking something out. Less is more. If the email is particularly important, read it out loud—or say the words silently. You'll be surprised at the mistakes you will want to correct.

It takes one more keystroke to add color to your email. I always do. Words in color make the message appear unique and can increase the interest level.

TIMELESS WISDOM

Your communication *is* your message. Form is as important as substance. Upgrade your communication and brighten your image.

23

Ask Questions and Listen, Please

*It is necessary for the general
to make correct estimates of the enemy's situation
to create conditions leading to victory.*
—Sun Tzu

 In order to make correct estimates of any situation, we must gather information. In order to gather information, we must ask questions and listen to the answers. Correct estimates cannot be made in interchanges in which we do most of the talking or take actions that impede the flow of information. You must ask your way to information by asking questions so that you can create the conditions leading to victory.

You can cast this truth in concrete:

- *The sale is not made by talking.*
- *The sale is made by listening.*

It's a fact: The more we listen, the more we can learn about our prospects and the easier it is to find their "hot buttons." It's not what we say that makes the sale; it's what we can get the prospect to say. The more we listen to why the customer wants to buy, the more we can tailor our delivery to how our product or service fills his or her needs.

It's a paradox: The more we try to tell the prospect, the more barriers we can create to the purchase. The more the prospect tells us, the closer we are to the answers.

QUESTIONS ARE THE ANSWER

Asking questions is a great way to improve your listening skills and win agreement. Get prospects to give you the answers; they will feel better and be more convinced by their answers than with your dialogue. If you can get the prospect to say what you want to say, his or her statement has more credibility than yours.

Socrates said that the only reason you talk in dialogues is to prepare the way for a question. Questions keep you in control. Think about when Johnny asks Dad for the car. A refusal creates the opportunity for more questions: "Why can't I have the car?" "Don't you love me?" The list goes on, and Dad gets frustrated because the questions are Johnny's attempt to put himself in a controlling position.

Asking questions leads you to uncovering information and keeps you in control. Why talk when you can learn so much by listening to answers to your questions.

When a company president told me that he needed to go to another city to talk to the staff of a newly acquired company about a problem they had raised, I asked, "What is the list of questions you want to ask?" It's basic to winning: The person who asks questions is in control of the discussion. The person who is in control often wins.

In selling situations, customers are frustrated when we ask a question to which they do not know the answer, and they are pleased when we ask a question to which they do know the answer. So act accordingly.

At the most basic level are two kinds of questions:

- *Open questions.* An open question encourages the customer to respond freely. It's the "tell me more" kind of question. Open questions probe for needs and background information.
- *Closed questions.* Closed questions can usually be answered by a yes, a no, or an alternative.

A large menu of variations can be derived from these two types of questions. The names applied to variations indicate their nature: directive questions, alternate choice questions, or reflective questions.

My personal favorite is the reflective question, which you use to simply reword (reflect) the other person's comment by making it your question. For example, when the other person says, "It won't work," repeat the sentence in the form of a reflective question—"It won't work?"—in a quiet but puzzled tone. With this approach, you neither accept nor deny the objection. Rather, you stand firmly in the same place and ask for more information. The reflective question merely inquires while giving you thinking time.

Be a sponge—gather information. You can't gather much information when you are doing all the talking. Never stop listening.

The U.S. Census Bureau uses a questioning approach that can work for you. One of the problems census takers encounter is getting women to state their true age. Here is an interchange that works. At a home interview, the census taker uses the following question sequence:

Q: "Who is the head of the household?"
A: "James Jones. He's at work now."
Q: "Is Mr. Jones married?"
A: "Yes."
Q: "What is his wife's name?"
A: "Jane Marie Jones."
Q: "What is Mrs. Jones's age?'
A: "Forty-two."

Note that "your age" is not asked. From this interchange, you may find the kernel of an idea for getting more information from your prospects.

PRACTICE ACTIVE LISTENING

We were born with two ears and one mouth for a reason. But don't just listen with your ears; listen with your entire body. Be an active listener. Take notes, if appropriate—and let the prospect observe that you are interested enough to take notes. Taking notes of what is said keeps you actively involved and focused on what is being said.

Use body language, and your listening habits will automatically improve. Lean forward intently. Look the prospect in the eye and focus on the valuable information you are hearing. Listen for buying signals that tell you the prospect is ready to act.

Here are a few rules for listening that apply equally well in one-on-one and group situations:

- If we keep our mouths closed, our ears are more liable to be open.
- Listen intently. Concentrate. Maintain eye contact. Have good body posture. A physically alert stance keeps us mentally alert.
- Be careful not to interrupt the speaker. This disruption of the thought process is irritating.
- Whenever possible, structure the selling situation to avoid outside interruptions or distractions.
- Mirror the speaker. Smile when he or she smiles. Nod when the other person nods.
- Measure input. Afterward, think about how much each person talked. Dividing the meeting time by the number of people present gives the average talking quotient. Compare the quotient to your own speaking time.

- Use participants' names frequently. This strengthens your relationship and increases the level of attention you receive. This technique works well one on one and in group situations.
- In groups, call on quiet members. Ask their opinion. Get the comments that will be made after the meeting out in the open. A simple "Frank, what is your reaction to this idea?" is a nonthreatening way to draw out information.

Good interactive communication phrases are:

"What I heard you say was . . . ." This paraphrasing of the other person's words captures his or her attention and clarifies the communication.

"What I want you to hear is . . . ." This technique is more directive and might be used with a chuckle in a sales conversation to emphasize something that would be of special interest to the customer.

BEGIN BY LISTENING

It's important, very important, to start the listening process at the beginning of the sale.

Why is it that new salespeople, or experienced salespeople who have a new product or service, want to do all the talking? The reason is that they are afraid the prospect will ask them a question to which they don't know the answer.

One evening in Kalamazoo, Michigan, I had dinner with one of my salespeople. Engaging in role playing, I said, "Jim, sell me on our franchise." I clocked 27 minutes of continuous presentation. I can't say that I listened during the entire time because the normal attention span is about 3 minutes. Finally, in desperation, I interrupted and asked, "Jim, why didn't you ask me a question? For example, Do I think I could increase my profits with our franchise?" He said, "Jerry, I thought you'd say 'No.'" The sale begins when the customer says "No." This was a golden opportunity to remind Jim of the importance of questions as a means to listening.

I can't tell you how many times I thought I knew what the customer wanted and launched right into the presentation. Some time later, often too much later, I've found out that what I was selling wasn't what the prospect wanted to buy. He or she had an entirely different need I could have uncovered by asking questions requiring more than a "Yes" or "No" response—open questions like, "What's your main objective?" or "What's the major problem you need solved?" Then I could have focused on what the customer wanted to buy instead of what I had to sell.

Never stop listening. If your organization isn't doing follow-up surveys with customers and former customers, get that engine started.

When doing group presentations, don't let the brevity of answers to your questions throw you off balance. Some group members can be unsure of their roles. If the boss is sitting in the back row, this may generate fear in some participants.

Some customers want to hear what you have to say first. That's fine. Adapt your presentation style to their request. Ask for a clarification of how your product meets their needs after completing your presentation.

Make active listening with open questions a hallmark of your normal style. This ensures getting the maximum information from each presentation.

WHY "WHY?" IS A BAD QUESTION

If you want to get to the reason behind the customer's resistance, "Why?" is the wrong question. The word sounds as if you are arguing and asking for justification of a position. I can vividly recall an army first sergeant growling, "Privates don't ever ask why; only generals ask why."

For example, when the prospect says, "Your price is too high," don't ask "Why?" Instead ask a question such as, "What price range are you considering?" When the prospect says, "I don't think your product will work," don't ask "Why?" Instead say, "What is it that gives you that impression?"

The best approach is always to move away from the threatening "Why?" to trying to coax out the reason behind the customer's comments.

KEEP ON LISTENING

Sure, we want to talk, so that the prospect will learn how smart we are. The prospect *really* knows that we are smart when we have "listened" to the information he or she wants to share. The prospect really knows that we are smart about subjects important to him or her when the *prospect* has imparted that information.

You can think more than four times as fast when you are listening than when you are talking. Strive for the listening advantage.

Beware of that terrible tendency to try to get your point in as soon as the customer stops talking. I've found myself stepping in before the customer had finished making his or her point. By stepping on the customer's last words, I was telegraphing that I wasn't listening and therefore appeared impolite. I was so intent on saying what I wanted to say that I didn't really hear what was being said by the customer. Since I interrupted the customer's presentation, he or she probably was not receiving what I had to say.

HAVE A THIRD EAR

The "third ear" is found between the lines. While listening to what is being said with both ears, use the third ear concept to observe the speaker's body language and evaluate what's not being said. This helps you understand his or her motives, decision-making authority, and emotions underlying the sale.

You have found the advantage of the third ear when you mentally dig into the reasons underlying what is being said. This is where the gold is buried.

TIMELESS WISDOM

I know I've had a bad sales experience when I've done all the talking. When I've done the talking, I haven't learned the "shape" of my prospect's needs. Active listening is what selling is all about.

24
Turn Problems into Opportunities

The commander must create a helpful situation
over and above the ordinary rules.
—Sun Tzu

 If there were no problems, there would be no need for people who could solve them. The task of the salesperson is to provide solutions for customers' problems—or for problems customers do not know they have or are going to have.

Finding problems is what prospecting is all about. The real estate salesperson focuses on finding people who have the problem of buying or selling a house. The insurance salesperson turns the problem of family security into an opportunity. People selling computer software are often plowing new ground when they provide solutions.

IDENTIFYING PROBLEMS

In large organizations, getting a good read on problems can be a challenge. Potential prospects may not be forthcoming with their problems. They may be worried about information getting to competitors, peers, or senior management.

Here are ways to find the information that leads you to the right questions:

- Read quarterly and annual reports. It is amazing how infrequently this is done. Look for insights into core strengths. Search for the current buzzwords—they may be in the president's message. Being familiar with corporate reports can give you a great opportunity to quietly demonstrate that you have done your homework.
- Search out the prospects' most successful products or services. This knowledge can come from the reports and from others in their industry. Being able to pass on a compliment from a customer is more proof of having done your homework and can open up opportunities to talk about your prospects' successes.
- Start with a known industry problem. If you can show knowledge of the problem and can offer solutions, you have a dynamite opportunity. Appeal to the buyer's desire to be the person who finds solutions that increase the organization's profits.

A PROBLEM IS AN OPPORTUNITY

When selling a product through retailers, we always publicized our biggest sales event of the year in the local newspapers. On one occasion, in my major market the newspapers went on strike just as the ads were to break. By purchasing large blocks of advertising time on the local television stations and reselling the time to local retailers, we turned the problem into an opportunity. In fact, we purchased enough time to become the dominant advertiser in our product category. Temporarily, we owned the media link to the customer. The result was the biggest sale ever. The big problem bred our biggest opportunity.

While traveling, I met two Australian merchants who were taking other people's problems and turning them into opportunities. They were making their fortune finding surplus products in one country and selling them in another. They found the best opportunities in countries emerging into the free world.

DO AN OPPORTUNITY SEARCH

If you don't have a problem, find one so that you can profit from the opportunity. The old adage "If it ain't broke, don't fix it" has been replaced by a new one: "If it ain't broke, you haven't looked hard enough."

TIMELESS WISDOM

In every problem is an opportunity. The key to finding the opportunity lies in thoroughly analyzing the problem. Discovering the solution is not an easy task; that's why a problem is a problem.

The Second Step:
MAXIMIZE THE NEED

Identifying the need is not enough; help your prospect understand the ultimate level of benefits over time.

Help your customer realize the lifelong value of your product or service. Spending a little more can mean a lot. Talk about the daily or weekly extra pleasure or value. If the extra value of your product or service is $1000 a month, that is equal to $12,000 a year and $120,000 over 10 years. Wow!

The cost of a product or service spread out over its lifelong use can be reduced to pennies a day. In selling to end users, this can be compared to the cost of a cup of coffee a day. In selling to industrial buyers, this cost can be reduced to a low annual hourly rate over the life of a product.

Don't shortchange your value; express it in terms of a daily benefit over a span of time.

25
Scope It Up—or Down

When torrential water tosses boulders, it is because
of momentum.
The energy is similar to a fully drawn crossbow.
The timing is similar to the release of a trigger.
—Sun Tzu

 Scope is a "torrential" process for amplifying benefits to the maximum and reducing costs to the ridiculous. Scope builds a powerful momentum in the sale. When you scope it up, maximize the benefits. When you scope it down, reduce the costs of your product or service to the lowest common denominator.

Here is how scope works.

SCOPE IT UP

To scope it up, multiply the annual benefit by the useful life of the product. For example, $100,000 extra profit over a span of 10 years is $1,000,000.

One of my top salespeople would sell our franchise by asking a prospect, "How would you like to make a million dollars?" That was the amount of profit the prospective customer could expect to make on our franchise over his or her lifetime. The salesperson would validate his or her claim by working out the annual profit and multiplying the annual profit by the number of years remaining before the prospect might sell his or her business. For example, $50,000 per year over 20 years equals $1,000,000.

SCOPE IT DOWN

To scope it down, apply the same principle to costs. For example, an investment of $100,000 averages only $10,000 a year over a 10-year time span. (Note that the *cost* becomes an *investment*.) Divide by the number of weeks in the year to arrive at less than $200 a week, which is less than $30 a day

My star sales professional used the technique of scoping cost down to sell retailers on erecting outdoor signs with the name of our product. After all, a giant $15,000 sign would attract a lot of attention. It would last 10 years, and the average investment would be only $1500 per year, or about $4 per 24-hour day. The street would be busy with potential prospects about 15 hours each day, so the hourly investment could be illustrated with a quarter coin. My star sold lots of signs, and the signs sold lots of product.

An extra investment of $1000 over a 4-year life span averages $250 a year, or $5 a week, or 70 cents a day. Compare the 70 cents a day to the price of a cookie. Balance the investment against the extra benefits that can be enjoyed for cookies per day. Wow!

SCOPE WORKS!

Scope is useful to anyone selling anything. I've used scope to maximize the benefits of a capital investment and again, in the next minute, to minimize the costs. I've seen scope reduce the cost of a multi-million-dollar training program for a large corporation to a low daily investment per participant.

SUN TSU: STRATEGIES FOR SELLING

When possible, express the lowest unit daily investment in ridiculous terms like the cost of a Big Mac or an order of french fries.

Scope up to maximize the positive—such as savings or value. Scope down to minimize the negative—such as investment, time, or distance.

TIMELESS WISDOM

Scope is a simple process. Multiply benefits to the max; reduce costs to the ridiculous.

26
Tip the Scales

The commander who gets many scores
during the calculations in the temple before the war
will have more likelihood of winning.
—Sun Tzu

 After completing a tour of a silver mine in the mountains of Colorado, I asked the old prospector to sell me a dollar's worth of silver dust.

He got out a set of old-fashioned balance scales and put a silver dollar on one side. The empty side rose high in the air. Then he began pouring silver dust on the empty side. When the two sides of the scale were evenly balanced, I knew I had a dollar's worth of silver dust.

However, he did not stop pouring the precious dust, and soon the side with the dust was tipped way over—in my favor. I knew that I had more than a dollar's worth of silver dust—a real value. I wanted to leave with my silver dust before he took some back.

GET MANY SCORES

The selling process is much the same. Your product or service is on one side of the scale, and your dialogue with the customer determines the value of the benefits on the other side. When the customer's perceived value of the benefits equals the price of the

119

product or service, you can have a sale. If you can tip the scales way over, with an abundance of perceived value for the customer, you can have a sale much more easily—and a happier customer. Happy customers are repeat customers.

The extra value helps overcome the buyer's remorse that can set in after a purchase is made. When we get a really good deal, we are less likely to want to return the purchase. When we are in possession of a great value, our biggest concern is keeping the purchase—not taking it back.

We win when customers believe they are getting more than their money's worth. In measuring the value of the benefits, the customer's perception is the reality.

If we look at the weight of benefits only from our perception, we may lose the sale. What counts is the customer's perception. Our job is to help the customer judge value. In order to do our job well, we must understand value from the customer's point of view.

After we completed the purchase of a new car one Christmas, the dealer asked us to take an envelope off the Christmas tree. He explained that these envelopes contained gifts ranging from $100 to $500 for his best customers. We were so impressed at being a best customer that not only did we return years later to buy another car, we recommended his dealership to friends.

YOUR VALUE ADDED

The way to winning is bringing added value to your customers. Some of this added value is you; some is your company. Load up the scales with the added value important to your customer. What makes the sale sizzle is the personal added value from you or your team. What's critical to the customer is not just what your product or service will do; it's the value you personally add with the promise of a continued service relationship. Find opportunities that enhance your value. Keep in touch with the customer. Call headquarters and enlist your team in this effort.

The mantra in fast foods is QSVC—that is, *quality*, *service*, *value*, and *cleanliness*. Each chain strives to excel in these areas. A drugstore chain has adopted the name CVS. You guessed it. The initials stand for *convenience*, *value*, and *service*. Unfortunately, the company markets the initials, so the significance of the words is lost.

What is your mantra for your personal added value? Certainly you want quality and service. How about the personal value from *knowledge* and *relationship*?

As Sun Tzu says, "The commander with many scores will have more likelihood of winning."

Timeless Wisdom

Bring a personal value into your relationships—beyond what you bring as a representative of your company. This requires an extensive knowledge of your business and industry.

Third Step:
FILL THE NEED

Selling has been defined as an interchange in which the salesperson and prospect think through a proposition in relation to the prospect's needs and arrive at a mutually profitable decision.

Filling the prospect's need is closing the sale. Books written about the close portray it as some magical moment when we get the customer to say, "Yes" and then go on our way. That's not the way it works in the real world. Good sales professionals are always asking for the order by continually serving the customer. The decision to buy is the result of a chain of interactive experiences.

APPEAL TO EMOTIONS

Some people think that the customer's decision to buy is a logical decision. Most often, it's not. The decision to buy is an emotional decision. The emotion often has little to do with price; it has to do with the benefit of the features. Appealing to the emotions helps support the price. That's a big reason why we pay more for high-quality brand names.

To succeed, you have to get into the customer's heart. The way to do that is with emotion—the power that gets people to act.

Logic and hard facts appeal to common sense and visible needs. Logic and facts are the skeleton of a successful sale. They must be clothed in flesh and nurtured by the warmth of a beating heart. Emotions make logic and facts come to life when they arouse the heart. Emotions are what move people to make decisions.

The great motivating force in every transaction is finding some way to gain a benefit or avoid a loss. As discussed earlier, scope maximizes these forces. Sometimes, the deciding emotional benefit is clear, as when Andrew Carnegie sold George Pullman on the idea of merging their sleeping car interests. After hearing the logic and facts, Pullman asked, "What would the new company be called?" Ever sales-oriented, Carnegie replied, "The Pullman Company, of course."

I learned about emotion in buying decisions one winter day when I was traveling in Oregon, calling on established accounts and selling a new design of a proven product. To each customer, I made a very logical presentation about how the new product variation would sell. In the town of Klamath Falls, the owner was ill and the buying decision was to be made by another person. After I finished my carefully prepared and thoroughly rehearsed presentation, which had worked so well elsewhere, I got the response, "I agree with everything you say, but I don't like the design and I'm not going to buy the product."

Later, as I thought about why I didn't make that sale, I realized that an emotional reaction was at work. I had not sold to the other buyers using a presentation based on logic. They bought not because of logic but because of their faith (an emotion) in my advice based on a long relationship. I had no credibility (an emotion) with the new buyer.

We do make rational presentations to which it appears that we get a logical decision. Underlying this logical decision is an emotional base.

In the business-to-business sale, this emotional base is the desire of buyers for success so that they can keep their jobs, get a raise, get promoted, or be recognized for the worth of their decisions. A different emotion underlies the sale to entrepreneurs who own a small business. Corporate buyers see the sale as a business transaction with benefits that could make them heroes; entrepreneurs see the cost coming directly from the profits they want to earn to fulfill their dreams.

In the sale to end customers, the emotional nature of the transaction is readily apparent. We see it most often in the reaction to style when the customer says simply, "I like it" or "I don't like it."

Some decisions need time for the mind to review the situation. People are often convinced more by the passage of time than by facts. Allow time for internal emotions to work.

The best sales results happen when we recognize the importance of understanding and appealing to the emotions.

SELL THE DIFFERENCE

Often, we don't need to sell the whole enchilada; what we need to sell is the extra value of our product or service.

Don't get trapped by selling the entire cost of the product or service. Price discussions should cover the price differential between your product or service and another product or service the customer is considering.

The prospect is spending his or her income on something. Find out what he or she is thinking about buying, and then sell the difference between the cost of that product or service and the one you have to offer.

Focus on the extra value that differentiates your product or service. This difference can be in lower cost to acquire, in lower operating cost over time, or in extra value features and benefits.

Selling the difference can be a great opportunity to apply scope, because all you need to scope is the difference. Scope can really work to your advantage, because you can scope up the benefit difference while scoping down the cost difference.

MAKE ALL DECISION MAKERS HEROES

The larger the corporate purchase, the more likely that several people must say "Yes."

The best way to eat this elephant is to cut it up into little pieces. Different buying influencers have different needs that need to be considered.

Top-level decision makers focus on the economic benefits of the transaction. These executives are measured by profit and want to know how the product or service affects the bottom line. In your discussion, think about what the chief executive officer might say to the board of directors about the purchase. When required, the CEO's favorable decision is vital to sales success.

The user-buyer wants to know how your product or service helps him or her succeed in the job. Get a "Yes" here, and you have a strong influencer working for you.

Staff departments are interested in whether your product or service meets the technical specifications. They are screeners. Their "Yes" opens the gate; their "No" is a deadly rejection.

Enlist the aid of your coaches in learning the positions and needs of all who will influence the buying decision. Do not depend only on discussions and presentations to make your points. Follow up with letters summarizing critical points to key influencers. Find ways to keep in touch with every level.

"Don't sell what doesn't work. Making a sale today that fails tomorrow poisons the well of future opportunities. There is no greater sin in selling than making a sale that loses the customer. When the customer is disappointed in the results of the product or service, you have destroyed future business and opportunities for references. Just as people talk about what they like, people talk about what they do not like. And, if they really do not like it, they talk more often to more people."

27
Offer a Unique Selling Proposition

*The law of successful operations is to
avoid the enemy's strength and strike weakness.*
—Sun Tzu

 If your product or service is just like your competitor's, your competitor will probably eat your lunch. Find a unique selling proposition (USP) that differentiates your product or service and match it to a customer who wants that differentiation.

The Unique Selling Proposition is a feature or benefit that not only avoids the opponent's strength, it emphasizes your strength while striking at the opponent's weakness. For example, if the feature in a new car is a sensor that signals when you are backing into something, the benefit is avoiding accidents and costly repairs. If you are selling the only brand (or one of a few brands) that has this feature or benefit, you have a unique selling proposition.

SEARCH FOR THE BEST USP

Having the lowest price isn't a very good USP, because an even lower price can beat your low price. The best USP is one that can't be easily copied or duplicated. If you don't have a

127

USP, you have a product or service that might be classed as a commodity.

TURN PROBLEMS INTO
USP OPPORTUNITIES

Here's how my friend Alice Rutten, a very successful real estate broker, overcame obstacles by "imagineering" a USP that could be matched to the customer.

Alice was approached by a tile contractor who wanted to sell his house. Other real estate brokers had looked at the house and decided that it wasn't very marketable because there was too much tile. Alice told me, "This house didn't just have tile in the kitchen and bath; it had tile all over the house. Some rooms had tile ceilings."

Alice knew that tile was her Unique Selling Proposition and that only someone who appreciated the value and craftsmanship of tile would be interested in this house. After completing the selling agreement, she called the tile contractors listed in the Yellow Pages and found a buyer even before she finished calling all the names on the list.

On another occasion, Alice was faced with the "opportunity" of selling a house near the railroad tracks in an affluent suburb. She says, "There wasn't any way you could ignore the existence of the railroad tracks. They were right in front of you when you drove down the driveway. I decided that the only people who would buy this house would be people who liked trains."

Trains on the railroad tracks became the USP. Alice ran an ad appealing to people who like trains. The house sold quickly to a family who had lived near railroad tracks and liked the experience. When Alice stopped by one evening to take the new owners to dinner, the children said that, as a reward for being good, they were being allowed to stay up to watch the 9 o'clock train.

When the product cannot be changed, it is the task of the sales professional to be creative and find a USP that can be matched to the right customer.

TIMELESS WISDOM

The Unique Selling Proposition is the sales professional's friend. It is your task to match the uniqueness of your offering to the customer. This is selling at its finest.

28

Do the Extraordinary

*Use the normal force to engage;
the extraordinary to win.*
—Sun Tzu

 Focusing on the extraordinary is one of the most useful ideas from Sun Tzu.

Little bits of effort get little bits of results. In selling, we often attempt to achieve extra sales by searching for more resources—if only we had more time, more prospects, more customers, or more price reductions.

Too many sales plans accomplish little more than a slight skirmish with the competitor and no significant increase in position with the customer. Forget the ordinary; plan for a breakthrough. Only sales plans involving extraordinary effort achieve extraordinary success.

A little more effort than last year often yields the same results as last year because competitors are also improving. It takes a lot of practice to hit a home run or make a touchdown. But that's the way games and sales battles are won—by efforts that can yield extraordinary results.

MAKE AN
EXTRAORDINARY EFFORT

Working hard does not guarantee extraordinary results. Working hard works only when you work on the right things. Working smart—on the right things—gets results. The customer is the only person who can tell us whether we are properly focused, and we'll get that message only if we are listening.

I am amazed at how many times I've heard the statement of a solution to a problem begin, "The easiest thing to do would be . . . ." The easiest thing to do is not what gets the most sales. Too many others are doing the easiest thing. How many times do we find the same item in store after store? Duplication of inventory provides no differentiation and opens the door to profitless price wars.

In a town in Michigan is a shoe store that stocks a wide variety of sizes of the same shoes. Everyone who enters the store is always greeted by a salesperson. You probably can find the shoe you want in your size. Throughout the state are countless shoe stores stocking only the most popular sizes and selling them at a discount. No discounts are offered in this unique shoe store because it is not selling what everyone else has.

A SALES FABLE

Stony Whittaker from Bell Buckle, Tennessee, was the star salesperson of the year in a territory where his predecessor had quit in disgust, sending back the message, "There's no potential here. Everyone goes barefoot." After a few months in the new territory, Stony advised, "There's a tremendous potential here. Everyone goes barefoot."

At the next national sales meeting, Stony was asked to deliver a presentation about his success. When Stony stepped up to the podium, he saw all the people in the audience and got stage fright. All he could mumble into the microphone was his reaction: "See the people, see the people." And then he sat down. After a moment of silence, the audience burst into thunderous applause because they realized that in those few simple words Stony had captured the essence of success: "See the people."

Making calls to see all the people requires an extraordinary effort that can generate extraordinary results.

THE IMPORTANT EXTRA

The difference between first and last place in most endeavors is a few percentage points. The difference between first and second place in Olympic races can be measured in fractions of an inch or in hundredths of a second. In selling, the difference between winning and losing is often the result of a little extra effort.

In baseball, assuming that a player gets 500 at bats during the season, a .300 hitter gets 150 hits and a .250 hitter gets 125 hits. Just one extra hit a week over the course of a season separates the star from the mediocre player.

I have found that one extra customer contact every day makes a big difference in my results over time. That one extra contact each day adds up to 20 a month and 250 a year. That's a lot of extra networking working for you. If you can't make one extra call a day, even half that rate can generate a higher level of success.

Of course, you must determine where that extra time and energy investment will get the best results. Perhaps, you should invest that extra time with high-potential regular customers. Be warned that is the easy thing to do; the hard thing to do is to call on new prospects.

The something extra might be time invested in your profession. I've met great salespeople who tell me that they get up early to study their industry and profession. I've never been a really early riser, but I've often been a late-night student.

The only thing that stands in the way of our success is us. Don't be like the person leaning against the lamppost watching successful people go by and saying, "There but for me go I."

GIVE EXTRAORDINARY ATTENTION TO YOUR CUSTOMERS

Every year I've sent Thanksgiving cards to customers. I learned that idea from a retail salesman in the state of Washington who sent Thanksgiving cards containing a handwritten verse in the days before Thanksgiving cards were readily available. Thanksgiving cards work better than Christmas cards because greeting cards at Thanksgiving stand out from the clutter of Christmas cards. My surveys at sales conferences indicate that very few people receive more than five Thanksgiving cards, and most are from relatives. It's amazing how many people will comment that they appreciated your Thanksgiving card.

Secretaries' Week is a great occasion for a gift. A small box of candy around Halloween can make a big impression. Stopping in with a treat goes over big anytime. In today's more diet-conscious times, I've found that boxes of a new kind of snack cracker or miniature cookies are well received. You get the best results with something new because it arouses interest and makes it look as if you are knowledgeable about what's new.

Think about what concerns your customer the most and concentrate on relieving the anxiety. The action might be a phone call to advise the customer that the order has been shipped or an idea that helps his or her business. The point is to keep on being the one who delivers extra interest and value.

Sometimes I've found that just responding promptly and being readily available is enough to be considered special. This is because so few people understand the basic idea of being really interested in serving the customer. It takes something extra, but not very much, to separate ourselves from the masses. Little things *do* mean a lot.

TIMELESS WISDOM

Special customers are those who are treated like special customers. Special treatment comes from you. Do not delegate this important task.

29
Work the Advantages

A skilled commander sets great store
by using the situation to the best advantage.
—Sun Tzu

 You can find advantages in every situation. The customer's objection is not bad news; it is good news because the objection is a request for more information. How difficult it is when the customer says nothing and does not voice his or her thoughts. The objections you never hear are the ones that kill the sale. The discussion about the objection is an opportunity to exercise your persuasion skills.

Here are ways to handle the transition from a "No" to a "Yes."

AGREE

Steve Gissin of Auragen Communications in Rochester, New York, uses the term *forness* to describe the attitude of being in agreement. He encourages staff to be *for* ideas of others because forness helps one to find the strength of an idea and build on it. Gissin's appeal for an upbeat attitude is a useful example of how a positive approach can help build opportunities.

When receiving the prospect's objection, always respond with a positive comment that accepts the worth of the objection.

The prospect raised the objection because he or she thought that it was a good idea—or perhaps, a good excuse to keep from making the purchase. Disagreement signals the beginning of an argument. Argue, and you will often lose. An argument becomes a clash of egos, with each side digging into its position. The longer you argue, the more each side digs into its position; extending the time dimension creates depth. Remember the long feud and the depth of hatred between the Hatfields and the McCoys? Agreement is the start of a discussion—a calm, thoughtful, and informative exploration of ideas. Here's how you can win by combining an attitude of "forness" with an expression of "yesness":

> *"Yes, I understand how you feel . . ."*
> *"Yes, I can see your point of view . . ."*
> *"Yes, you do have a point . . ."*
> *"Yes, that could be a good reason . . ."*
> *"Yes, you are absolutely right . . ."*

Other ways to express the worth of the objection are

> *"Thank you for being so sincere . . ."*
> *"I'm glad you brought that up . . ."*

Select a few of these examples and make them common phrases in your vocabulary.

Be careful: Too often the above phrases are followed by that awful word *but*, as in "Yes, I understand how you feel *but* . . .

You might just as well have said "No, I don't understand how you feel." The *but* defeats the customer. Only goats butt. Buts lead you in the wrong direction. Add a *but* to any sentence, and out pops an argumentative statement. Use the connecting word *and* to lead you from a "Yes" to a positive statement. For example: "You certainly have a point, *and* it is worth considering."

The first component of the response accepts the worth of the other person's comment. Complete the response by requesting more information using open inquiries such as "Tell me more," "Could you explain more fully?" or "I want to hear . . . ."

Your objective is to keep the other person talking. You are doing that by advising that he or she made a good point. The other person will be pleased with your acceptance of the comment. You will have disarmed his or her ego. Your input will be viewed as constructive. Now you are on the side of the prospect, and in that position you can be a counselor. No longer are you viewed as an adversary.

Asking more questions to define the objection often leads you to a solution to the objection. Sometimes, the other person simply explains away his or her own objection.

It is true that objections are really requests for more information and that your best response to an objection can be a request for more information about the nature of the objection. After receiving the input, you can move on to answering the objection with phrases such as "Others have felt the same way, and . . . ."

"BRAG UP" THE OBJECTION

Often the objection can be turned into a positive. When the prospect says he or she has never heard of the product (or company) you might say, "Yes, that's understandable because the reputation of this product has been built through word of mouth and not advertising. The fact that the firm does not spend a lot of money on advertising is one reason why it is a good value." Then, present a testimonial or an entire portfolio of testimonials to support your position.

REVIEW A SIMILAR SITUATION

This scenario might be something like, "Yes, I can understand how you feel. John Jones had the same concern, and he checked it out and told me what he found. May I share his discovery with you?" Be careful: Do not give your opinion; tell what Jones said. Provide names and phone numbers.

OFFER HELP WITH "I'LL THINK IT OVER"

When customers say that they want to think it over, help them with their thinking. Take the customer through a list of possibilities covering why he or she is hesitating. For example, say, "That's a good idea. What do you want to think over? Is it delivery dates?" (Pause for an answer.) "Is it the product performance?" (Pause.) Continue with other possibilities. A word of caution: Do not pause to take a breath between the question "What do you want to think over?" and the first suggestion. If you do, the customer will say, "The whole thing!" Do not mention price early because the customer will say the price is too high. If you satisfy the customer on all the other points, the price objection will probably disappear.

There's another approach to "I'll think it over." You might respond with, "Yes, that's a good idea." Then add, "On a scale of one to five, based on what you know if you had to decide now, where would we be?" Let's assume that one means "No way" and five means "Absolutely." Of course, the answer will be less than five, so ask, "What would it take to make that number a five?" The response will often bring the hidden objection to the surface.

TIMELESS WISDOM

Have an attitude of "forness" and "yesness." Turn objections into advantages you can use to discover what's keeping the customer from buying.

30
Winning Is the
Best Option

*Throw them into a situation where there is no escape
and they will display immortal courage.*
—Sun Tzu

We have won and lost. Winning is a lot better.

STRIVE FOR EXCELLENCE

Approach each opportunity with the idea that you will give it
your best.

You and your customers don't want to be second best in anything. Can you recall the names of anyone who came in second in
anything? Focus on helping your customers win big time, and
you will win big time.

After I had spent a few years in the sales profession, a business
owner asked me what it took to make a good salesperson. I replied,
"You've got to be hungry and have guts." When probed for further information, I explained, "You've got to be hungry enough to
need the business and have enough guts to ask for the order."

Whatever product, service, or ideas you sell, having the hunger to win will help with the self-motivation that gives you the guts to do the right thing.

KEEP ON TRYING

On your way to winning, honor the difference between persistence and pestering:

Persistence is keeping in touch with the customer by using different techniques and influences to support your cause.

Pestering is using the same buying reason over and over again.

One of my favorite salespeople says, "I keep in touch with my customers until they buy or die." That's persistence.

Persistence works when you find a new benefit, offer different terms, or simply call back with a polite inquiry. Persistence is keeping in touch. Using the same approach or argument over and over again is the pressure of pestering—it doesn't work.

In a study of successful salespeople, the average successful salesperson made five attempts to close before getting the order. However, the closing question in each attempt took different forms.

As a young sales representative trying to sell a new major account, I can recall waiting outside the buyer's office for hours after the scheduled appointment time had passed and then returning the next day because the appointment had to be rescheduled. That persistence helped earn the order from a high-potential account.

Warning: If you are desperate to win the sale, there is a danger that you will transmit that desperation to the customer. Find an alternative outlet for your nervous energy.

TIMELESS WISDOM

Don't give up when you don't get the order on the first call. Each subsequent call means that you are that much closer to the goal. Keep looking for different ways to make the customer want to buy.

31
Be Flexible

*Tactics change in an infinite variety of ways
to suit changes in the circumstances.*
—Sun Tzu

 Flexibility in tactics is the keynote to success in selling. Flexibility doesn't mean that you give in to opposition; it does mean that you understand what the customer needs and adapt to those needs.

Recently, I participated in a selling interchange that reminded me of the old saying, "Turn on the green light, Mac. The guy wants a green suit." In this case, the customer did want a particular type of suit. However, it was not the one we had available. To make the sale, we had to listen carefully to the customer and adapt what we had to sell to the customer's perceived needs. Once again, the green light didn't work—what worked was the flexibility to redesign the "suit" so that it fit the customer's needs.

Customers learn to be more sophisticated from their own experiences. Henry Ford's "any color as long as it's black" worked until General Motors offered cars in colors. The hotels we might have stayed in 20 years ago are not very high on our list today unless they've continuously renovated the product and reinvented the service experience.

Old paradigm selling was based on taking what we had to sell and finding out where it could be sold. New paradigm selling identifies the needs of the customer and shapes the product or service to those needs. The best scenario is when customer needs have been revealed or validated by our own research.

HAVE ALTERNATIVES

Don't get trapped by relying on a single contact in a big organization. It's important to have a wide base of solid contacts at various decision-making levels in every customer's organization so that you have alternative avenues of approach when the inevitable personnel changes occur.

Sometimes it's a good idea to offer the customer alternatives so that choices can be made to meet needs.

Every presentation should have a back-up position. The thought process of thinking through alternatives often provides ideas that strengthen the presentation.

Every plan to achieve the sales plan should include backup plans. Things don't always go right. When planning to meet the sales target, plan to sell more than is required. I always develop plans to sell twice as much as the sales quota. That way, when I am only half as good as I think I am, I still make the sales plan.

I stumbled across this idea one year when I received a ridiculously high sales quota. I thought, "If headquarters is going to be that ridiculous, I will do the same." I scheduled meetings with my accounts to talk about the profit that would be earned with a major increase in sales. My message was "double your sales and triple your profits." It worked. I didn't have to worry about doubling volume the next year because I was promoted to sales manager. This promotion required a temporary cut in pay because sales managers often do not make a higher income than the top-earning sales professionals. My income climbed higher in the following years. In selling, there are two routes to the top and better income. One is as a top salesperson; the other is in top management.

Alternatives are necessary to meet the customer's changing needs. What customers want this month may be different from what they thought they wanted last month.

The alternatives you offer can be as simple as a choice of monthly payments instead of a lump sum or the opportunity to accept your proposal in two or three stages instead of the entire package. An alternative can be paying part in this fiscal year and part in the next fiscal year so that the budget from two fiscal years can be applied to the purchase price.

SEEK A BALANCE

The best plans have a combination of flexibility and rigidity. Like the trunk of a tree, certain fundamental issues must be rigid. The branches of a tree are flexible so that the tree can adapt to changing situations. For example, McDonald's has rigid standards for quality, service, value, and cleanliness. However, some flexibility is allowed in local marketing. On the Northeastern seashore, I've had a McDonald's lobster roll. In Wisconsin, where there is a strong German heritage, I've had a McDonald's bratwurst.

TIMELESS WISDOM

While focusing on a single route, always keep your eyes open for alternatives. Sometimes, a detour may be the best route to your objective.

32

Watch for Buying Signals

To direct a large army is the same as to direct a small one,
it is a matter of commands and signals.

—Sun Tzu

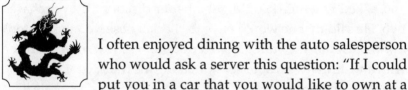 I often enjoyed dining with the auto salesperson who would ask a server this question: "If I could put you in a car that you would like to own at a price that you could afford, would you be interested?" Asking that question of someone he hardly knew was prospecting and qualifying rolled into one. No, he wasn't making the sale with that sentence, but he certainly was getting started.

Making a big sale is the same as making a small one; it is a matter of asking the kind of questions that lead to buying signals. When you hear or see a buying signal, go for it.

When the customer asks, "Can you?" as in "Can you change the color?" this is a buying signal. The correct answer to the customer's "Can you?" question is not "Yes" or "No." Most often, the correct response is some version of "If I can, will you (buy)?"

When the customer signals his or her interest with "Can you?" a "Yes" response means that you still have to ask for the order. Respond with questions like "If I can, do you want delivery tomorrow or the next day?" This gets agreement on the order. You have subtly asked whether your fulfillment of the request will result in a purchase.

If you already know that you can fulfill the request, the "If I can, will you . . .?" can be a great way to close the sale. If the customer agrees that fulfilling the request does indeed result in a sale, it may be best to arrange to call back with a response. An immediate affirmative response may make the agreement too transparent.

Immediate agreement may also create a situation in which the customer believes that his or her barrier was too easily overcome—resulting in the deadly disease of buyer's remorse. When I was shopping for a suit in a favorite store, the salesperson offered to give me the previous week's sale price. I found two suits I liked and asked whether I could get a better discount if I purchased two. He said that he would have to check. I observed that he took a walk around the store, looked out the window, and returned with an affirmative response. By making the transaction appear to require higher approval, he made it appear to be a better deal.

"If I can, will you . . .?" works best when the seller knows that the request can be fulfilled. It can be used also when you really do need to get approval from a higher authority—but only if you think it's the best course of action.

GETTING COMMITMENT

This is the test to determine whether you've uncovered enough needs. You want to move to an action that will close the sale. The action you suggest is determined by the type of commitment you are seeking. Here are commitments that might lead you to an agreement to purchase:

- Attending a demonstration
- Taking the product on trial
- Agreeing to the next meeting

- Allowing a needs analysis
- Requesting approval from a higher authority
- Introducing you to the decision maker

During your discussion, you should be using a sales aid called a *tie-down*. A tie-down is a brief question following a statement. It asks for agreement. For example, instead of "Is this what you want?" say, "This is what you want, isn't it?" The "isn't it" is the tie-down that follows a positive statement. It can lead you to the close or be the closing question. Other tie-downs are phrases such as "Don't you agree?" "Couldn't it?" "Wouldn't it?" or "Shouldn't it?" Be careful of tie-downs that become irritating speech habits. You hear them in frequently repeated words such as "Right" followed by another "Right" followed by a sentence ending in "Right." A repetitive "OK" is another overused tie-down.

The most important time to stop talking is after you've asked a closing question. After you've asked a closing question, the first person who talks loses. Because we can't stand the silence after asking a question, we stumble into the vacuum with a dumb comment that too often originates from insecurity and weakness. We think that the silence requires us to reinforce the weakest point, so we ask questions like "Is our price too high?" or "Perhaps you don't like the . . .?" Given an out (and a sign of weakness), the customer immediately responds, "That's it." Not only do you have more selling to do, but now you are selling from your weakness.

When you ask a buying question and then shut up, the customer can do only one of two things—either agree to buy or raise an objection.

My salespeople are always aware that the absolutely unbroken rule is that, after asking a closing question, they shut up! On joint calls we've sat in silence for minutes that seemed like hours, waiting for the prospect to say something. Afterward, we've chuckled together because we each knew what was going through the other's mind while we sat in silence. We knew the rule and knew that neither of us dared break the silence. There is no pressure in selling that equals the pressure of silence after asking a closing question.

In order for silence to work, be sure that a solid question has been asked like "Do you want delivery Wednesday or Thursday?" Saying "We can deliver on Wednesday or Thursday" is not a question.

ASSUMING AGREEMENT

Sometimes you can simply begin to fill out the standard order form. Ask the correct full name, the address, and so on. As long as you can keep going, the customer is signifying that he or she is buying.

The assumptive close is very important when the customer calls back on the phone or in person. The natural tendency is to ask whether he or she has thought it over. Since this can be the opening for the customer to voice a problem or objection, it's much better to move smoothly into the order-writing process immediately upon meeting or greeting the customer. This makes it necessary for the prospect to interrupt you if he or she isn't ready to buy.

OFFERING ALTERNATIVE CHOICES

The use of the alternative of choice always starts with "Which do you prefer?" and is followed by two choices. It might be "Which do you prefer, black or red?" or "standard or deluxe?" or "credit card or cash?" Always offer the other person a choice between doing things that are in your favor. For example, whether the prospect chooses cash or a credit card makes no difference to the salesperson. Never offer the prospect a choice between doing something and not taking action. If you do, the prospect will choose not taking action.

USING THE PUPPY DOG CLOSE

This close is used when the decision to buy is preceded by a decision to take the product home for a trial. When the product is a "puppy dog," the sale is made because no one ever returns puppy dogs. Think about how the trial of your product can be accompanied by a puppy dog that makes the sale.

I have always enjoyed my friend Martin Trout's variation of this one. In the days when washing machines weren't too common, Trout would stop by a prospective customer's house with a washing machine on his truck and offer to leave it with the homeowner for a demonstration. "No purchase is necessary," Trout would say. "I just have to get one more demonstration to make my quota for the month."

Trout would wait a few weeks and then stop at a neighbor's for coffee. During the discussion Trout would mention that he was on his way to a nearby house to pick up his demonstrator. "Oh," would be the reply. "I don't think you will need to pick it up. They want to keep it."

Trout would show up at his prospect's house and say that he was there to get his demonstration machine. With a friendly greeting, he would proceed immediately to the basement. Trout said, "The customers would stop me before I got the unit to the first step because they wanted to buy the washing machine." He never had to cut the price.

Nolan Bushnell used another variation of this close. Headquartered in San Francisco with the West Coast as his territory, Bushnell did his homework and determined which retailer he wanted to represent his wares in different towns in his territory. A retailer in Portland, Oregon, told me this story. He received a message stating simply, "Bushnell is coming." A few days later he received a message stating, "Bushnell is in Eureka." Each day he received another a message advising him of the progress of the mysterious Bushnell up the coast. One day the retailer received a large box marked, "Hold for Bushnell." Later, he received a message advising, "Bushnell will arrive at 2 PM on Wednesday."

Bushnell arrived promptly, asked for the carton, uncrated the product, made a demonstration, and franchised the account. How could anyone refuse this highly focused and determined sales approach!

ADDING UP THE BENJAMIN FRANKLIN BALANCE SHEET

When a prospect is trying to make a decision, tell this story: "Whenever Ben Franklin had a decision to make, he wanted to do the right thing—just as you do. Ben would take a sheet of plain paper and draw a line down the middle. Then Ben would put 'Yes' at the top of the left-hand column and 'No' at the top of the right-hand column. Then he would list all the reasons why he should and why he shouldn't make the decision. Finally, he would compare the results."

Turn the paper around so that it faces the prospect, hand him or her the pen, and say, "Let's think of all of the reasons why we should do this." Then help the prospect make a list of reasons for taking action. When this yes list is completed, ask the prospect to list the nos. At this point do not offer any assistance.

Of course, it's difficult for the prospect to write down the reasons why he or she shouldn't buy. Then it's a matter of counting the yeses and the nos.

FINDING A SIMILAR SITUATION

First, tell the customer about a similar situation when someone *didn't* buy and the problems that ensued as a result. Then, tell about a similar situation when someone *did* buy and the benefit that resulted. Then ask whether he or she would like to achieve similar benefits.

FOLLOWING UP ON THE LOST SALE

When you can't make the sale, ask the customer whether he or she would mind telling you why you lost the sale. When the customer tells you why, apologize for not covering that objection and explain it away.

CLOSING ON A MINOR POINT

Simply ask the customer a closing question and then follow with a minor question such as "Do you want to use your pen or mine?" or "Do you want delivery on Tuesday or Wednesday?"

THERE'S MORE

This is only an overview of the ways to bring the sale to a close. Entire books are filled with excellent information on closing. If you do all the other things well, the agreement to buy will be a natural outcome.

The important first step is generating leads to fill the funnel. Prospects are the lifeblood of the sale. After you have weeded out the prospects from the suspects, your focus should be on creating, maximizing, and filling the need.

TIMELESS WISDOM

Ask the right questions, and the prospect will give you the information that makes the sale.

33
Build Long Term

To win battle and capture lands and cities,
but to fail to consolidate these achievements is ominous
and may be described as a waste of time and resources.
—Sun Tzu

 Our definition of a great salesperson is not some-
one who just makes sales; a great salesperson
keeps on converting prospects into customers
who buy from that salesperson for life.

As professionals, we sell ourselves (the relationship), our
company, our product or services, and our value added. These
sales are never unsold because we keep on selling.

The sell-and-run approach does not work anymore. To differentiate themselves, some companies focus on their dedication
to providing service on their products.

In many cases, it's the software that sells the hardware. For
example, at the highway convenience store, systemwide software
controls the inventory. Because of the need for all stores to be
integrated, the store will purchase only hardware (such as a
gasoline pump) that is integrated with the system.

Customers want providers who can offer a full-range of solutions to their businesses. They want service from a team of peo-

ple who know their processes and requirements. The resulting relationship is referred to as a *partnership*. Often a formal partnership agreement is signed. Both parties enter into a win-win relationship and make a commitment to helping each other reduce costs.

That is, the supplier *wins* a steady customer, and the customer *wins* a supplier committed to cooperative relationships that reduce costs. The sales professional should be key to initiating and managing this partnership.

Here are guidelines for providing service to customers:

- *Be dependable.* Let your customers know where and how you can be reached. Return calls every day before the sun sets.
- *Keep in contact.* Calls to make sure that everything is going well are welcome and good business builders.
- *When things go wrong, leap into action.* This is the opportunity to prove your value to your customer.
- *Add value.* Be a conduit for new ways to get more value from your product or service.
- *Go the extra mile.* Figure out how to give the customer more than his or her money's worth.

Follow through on your commitment to satisfy your customers. The scrap heap you do not want is customers who will not come back. Work on keeping every customer you can possibly serve.

In a construction company office in Brinkley, Arkansas, a sign on the wall says, "Winners are willing to do things losers aren't willing to do." The owner isn't willing to lose any customer. She says, "When you win the customer who is tough to please, you earn your strongest supporter. These are the ones who will tell stories about the good work you do."

As the front line of contact, the sales professional should be the leader in stopping customer defections.

I often define a *customer* as someone you call to sell to and a *client* as some who calls you to purchase your services. That is not to imply that you wait for calls from clients. To keep clients, you must be actively in touch and getting feedback. Clients want to do business with you because they have had very good experiences with your services and believe you will help them improve their business.

TIMELESS WISDOM

Build long-term relationships. The best sales are those that are another step in turning customers into clients.

Part V

The Wisdom of Practical Experience

THE LAWS OF SELLING

- *The Law of the Customer—*
  The customer is king.
- *The Law of Expertise—*
  Get it.
- *The First Law of Prospecting—*
  Do it.
- *The Second Law of Prospecting—*
  Qualify.
- *The Law of Questioning—*
  Ask 'em.
- *The Law of Listening—*
  Shut up.
- *The First Law of Need—*
  Create it.
- *The Law of Scope—*
  Maximize it.
- *The Law of Benefits—*
  Have 'em.
- *The Second Law of Need—*
  Fill it.
- *The Law of Price—*
  Don't cut it.
- *The Law of the Order—*
  Ask for it.
- *The Law of Simplicity—*
  Keep it.
- *The Law of Lasting Relationships—*
  Go the extra mile.

The case studies on the following pages contain lessons from successful sales professionals who actively practice the laws of selling.

WISE LESSONS

Matthew Densen
General Manager, Norampac NYC Division

About 6 months after I started work as a cost estimator for a corrugated box manufacturer, the sales manager handed me some business cards and said, "Don't come into the office tomorrow. Go knock on some doors." That evening I purchased a briefcase, into which I dutifully placed my newly minted business cards and a tape measure.

The next day I drove to a local industrial park intent on becoming a sales success. As I recall, it took me about 45 minutes to get up the nerve to get out of the car and walk up to my first prospect. As I approached the door, another salesperson was leaving the office. On his way out, he said to me, "I hope you're not trying to sell corrugated boxes. That purchasing agent is a real jerk." So began my introduction into the art of selling.

I did get advice from company sales veterans. One said that a sure way to ferret out a good prospect was to follow a competitor's truck. I tried that twice. The first time I ended up in a competitor's truck yard. The next time I found myself parked behind a tractor trailer that pulled up in front of an apartment building. Over time I did discover more effective ways of identifying, contacting, and closing accounts. But it always seemed as though it was hit or miss. I didn't possess an organized, professional approach to selling, and my results always seemed to be inconsistent and random. Clearly, there had to be a better way.

When it was first suggested that my sales results could improve if I studied the works of a Chinese general who had been dead for two-and-a-half millennia, I was, to say the least, skeptical.

Sun Tzu teaches us: "War is a matter of vital importance to the State, a matter of life and death, the road either to survival

157

or to ruin. Hence it is imperative that it be thoroughly studied." Very few of us in our normal everyday lives will have to face the prospect of engaging in a fight to the death or have the burden of commanding troops in battle. Yet the lessons of Sun Tzu are as relevant to the successful salesperson today in the twenty-first century as they were to emperors and generals 2500 years ago. For those who seek to excel as professional salespeople today, *thorough study* is still imperative.

According to Sun Tzu, "The commander who gets many scores during the calculations in the temple before the war will have more likelihood of winning." By this we understand that superior planning and preparation are essential to victory. During my years as a sales manager and later as a leader of a company, I've had many opportunities to accompany salespeople on their first calls to prospective customers. When we arrived at our appointment, and before we left the car, I'd ask the following questions about the call we were about to make:

1. What is our mission? What is the purpose of this call? What do we hope to accomplish?
2. How do you intend to accomplish this mission? Specifically, how do you plan to proceed?
3. What is the best possible result we can expect to achieve with this call? What would you consider a home run?
4. How will we leave with an assignment? What will be the follow-up?

Unbelievably, many salespeople couldn't even begin to answer these questions even though we'd be only minutes away from walking into the prospect's office! Often a salesperson would answer that our goal was to get an order. Not a very realistic expectation for a first call.

A sales call, especially a first call to a prospect, should be thought out and planned as though it will be a major battle in which life and death hang in the balance. Like a general, a salesperson must have a clear objective in mind, a strategy on how to achieve that objective, and a precise knowledge of what constitutes victory. According to Sun Tzu, "A victorious army seeks its victories before seeking battle. An army destined to defeat fights in *hope* of winning." Successful salespersons have definite strategic goals in mind for every sales call. When a salesperson calls on a prospect for the first time, a winning strategy is to find the customer's needs.

The Art of War is concerned with preparing the general to prevail over the enemy. Good intelligence regarding the enemy's forces, its capabilities and deployment, is a necessary prerequisite to victory in battle. As Sun Tzu says, "Know the enemy and know yourself, and you can fight a hundred battles with no danger of defeat." Professional selling is no different.

At its core, the art of selling is determining the needs of the customer and then matching your capabilities and those of your organization with those needs. This is not always as straightforward a task as it sounds since many people, when asked what they *need*, will respond instead with what they *want*. Customers may be reluctant to divulge their real needs, fearing that in doing so they may be forfeiting a negotiating advantage.

Determining the customer's true needs is the salesperson's first strategic goal. Effective probing is a valuable tactic for achieving this goal. Asking questions that provide real intelligence about the customer's business is an essential basic skill of professional selling. Ask enough questions, and the customer will tell you what you need to do to sell him or her. A salesperson should maintain a list of at least 100 pieces of useful information about a customer and his or her business. For each piece of information in this list, design three or four possible questions to ask that will encourage the potential customer to talk about the business and its needs.

Clearly, it would not be effective, or appreciated by the customer, to rattle off a lengthy questionnaire. A handful of well-asked questions can provide a wealth of information about the customer's needs. Make sure the questions are open-ended so that the customer, not you, does the talking. Take notes to signal that what the customer is saying is important to you. Asking informed questions indicates you are serious about learning about the customer's business.

The need for accurate intelligence is not limited to finding out about the enemy. According to Sun Tzu, "If ignorant of both the enemy and yourself, you are sure to be defeated in every battle." A comprehensive understanding of your own company's capabilities and how they compare to the competition's is crucial if you are to successfully position yourself to defeat the enemy— in this case, the competition! Maintain a written evaluation of your competitors' strengths and weaknesses. Note where and how you've successfully competed against them and where they've beaten you out of business. This information will be invaluable when it comes time to design a strategy for addressing the customer's needs.

Knowing the customer's needs, your company's capabilities, and your competitor's strengths and weaknesses will put you in a good position to design a sales strategy to win the business. As Sun Tzu advises, "Use many to strike few at the selected place." Concentrate your efforts where you are more capable than your competitors, and avoid trying to compete where they are stronger.

Following Sun Tzu's advice has helped our company to consistently increase its market share in a very tough business. Implementing good selling tactics that support a sound marketing strategy has enabled us to survive many battles over the years. Occasionally, I'm still tempted to follow a competitor's truck when I see it on the highway, but I resist. I'm too busy working on real customers now, and besides, I've seen of enough of our competitors' truck yards!

ASSESS, UNDERSTAND, IMPLEMENT

Ann Staup, President
Direct Mail Services

When first exposed to applying military strategy to business by Gerald Michaelson in 1980, I must admit that the concept really didn't sink in. However, several years later, after participating in seminars on selling and marketing and reading more books than I can count, I finally get it. Actually, there are numerous books on those subjects that discuss goals, strategies, and tactics. The Sun Tzu books by Michaelson outline the groundwork necessary for success and provide the information in terms that are easily understood.

Assessing and understanding not only myself but also the needs and goals of employees and clients are essential in developing strategies and planning tactics. In my small company, the employees are the backbone of the operation. Instilling the correct practices and principles in everything they do, showing them how important they are to company success, and providing ongoing training help build the teamwork necessary to retain existing customers and acquire new ones. These activities are all a component of making them feel, no, making them know, that without them, no sale can be complete. Just as a general cannot succeed without his troops, no business can offer a quality product, provided in a timely manner, without trained, knowledgeable people.

Assessing the needs, goals, strengths, and weaknesses of the client provides the information necessary for success. Understanding the capabilities and services offered makes selling the service easy. But Sun Tzu teaches much more. Setting the goals, defining the challenge, developing the plan, and taking action

161

are explained in detail and in terms that are easy to understand and implement.

Just as in life, in business, integrity and professionalism are a must. Determining one's values, showing commitment, and being positive are keys to success. Knowing the competition, its weaknesses and strengths, is a must in establishing a position from which one can operate. Sun Tzu teaches us that, just as in a battle, what worked yesterday may not work today. Continuous learning and acquiring new insights provide a better ability to react to the challenges of today.

The principles of *The Art of War* are about understanding oneself, empowering others, and planning strategies and implementing the tactics necessary to succeed in business as well as life.

PLAN, SELL, AND WIN

Joseph G. Peca, Project Manager
Metso Automation USA

He who is well prepared
and lies in wait for an enemy who is not well prepared will win.
Throw them into a situation
where there is no escape and they will display immortal courage.
He who understands
how to handle both superior and inferior forces will win.
—Sun Tzu

How many times have we heard that it will take luck or a miracle to achieve a goal? In 1980, 20 college students under the guidance of a brilliant strategist achieved the unthinkable—the stunning upset by the U.S. Olympics ice hockey team over the Soviet Union's team. This improbable victory came less than 2 weeks after the Soviets blitzed the United States for 10 goals in a pre-Olympic exhibition contest. It was a miracle. It was luck. It was lightning in a bottle. On the contrary, it was a model of excellent management preparation in developing the strategy: successful selling of the concept to the team and methodical execution of the plan. It was pure Sun Tzu.

A professional hockey referee made a statement to me that I remember to this day: "Luck is nothing more than opportunity meeting preparedness."

I have been fortunate enough to experience personally the miracle and the luck in both my business career and my athletic coaching hobby. Having achieved these accomplishments before reading Sun Tzu, I now realize that my "miraculous and lucky" personal achievements were reached by unknowingly using several of Sun Tzu's concepts.

163

THE BUSINESS TEAM

The company I work for was awarded the largest domestic contract in our history. I was assigned as project manager and helped hand pick a select team to design and deliver a very complex, leading-edge hi-tech system. The product had not been developed, delivery penalties were high, and we needed to impress a new owner. We all knew that we had to succeed. I had to sell the team on doing what was necessary to get the job done, and I had to sell the customer on our performance.

The plan was developed. It was sold to the project team. The war was won because our company and the client achieved their respective goals. Little did I realize at the end of this project that I would be faced with a comparable and equally monumental challenge outside of my business career.

THE SPORTS TEAM

Coaching a high school ice hockey team was a struggle, but we qualified for the playoffs and were slotted as the fifteenth seed. When we competed with the number two seed, our defensive strategy worked to near perfection. Our weakest line complained about lack of ice time. Our opponent tied the game with 3 minutes remaining in the final period. We went into sudden death overtime and lost when I gave our least-skilled line a shift early in the overtime despite recommendations by my primary assistant to shorten the bench and just skate the top two lines. As my assistant told me the day after our loss, "You had the right system in place, but you coached with your heart in overtime." He nailed it. I had the equation half right. The plan was nearly perfect, but I had not sold the team on the sacrifices that we would need to make. I had felt obligated to use weaker players at the crucial point of the game.

I volunteered to coach for one more season. Our team was smaller in number and appeared weaker than the year before. In one midseason game we were whipped by an area private school, Archbishop Carroll, 10-0. (The game was ended early in the final period because of a mercy rule invoked when a team is losing by 10 goals.) After this game, we were at an all-time low. I was mad at the players; the players were mad at each other and me. Our goalkeeper was mad at the world.

I decided to add a handful of skilled, middle-school-age players. The kids finally began to buy into the system we were employing and the sacrifices we would have to make to progress in the postseason. Complaints about ice time diminished to a whisper and eventually ceased.

Our 10-2 demolishing of an opponent late in the regular season gave us confidence going into the playoff games. The playoffs looked formidable. We played as close to a perfect game as possible in round 1, winning 2-0. We shocked another opponent with four first-period goals, and they never recovered: we won 5-2.

We prepared for the final game the next night. Our opponent was Archbishop Carroll, the same team that dominated us by ten goals right before Christmas. I took a day off from work to prepare for the biggest game of my coaching career. Our opponent was undefeated and untied, with sixteen straight wins. We had eight wins along with six losses and two ties. To say we were facing an incredible challenge is the all-time understatement. It was a cold, rainy, miserable day, and I hoped that it was not an omen for the game. Our game plan was quite basic: play airtight defense, stick our best skaters against their best, stay close to the end, and capitalize on the few opportunities we would get. Our only advantage would be the element of surprise. Considering their regular season 10-0 win over us, they had to be taking us lightly.

When we arrived at the arena, the stands were packed. My son and I looked at each other in shock. A chat with the league commissioner revealed his surprise—he had to double-check to confirm that we really qualified for the championship game.

As we prepared to take the ice, our players and staff were serious but relaxed. These were good signs. The last thing we needed was to be so tense that we forgot what we needed to do. My pregame speech centered on the game plan, line matchups, and the 1980 U.S. Olympics team with its loss to the Soviets in an exhibition blowout followed by the upset in the tournament. I stressed that our opponents would remember the team they beat by 10 goals 3 months earlier. Their players and coaches would not be prepared to face our revamped team.

I advised the team that ice time would be dictated by the game situations and that nobody should take it personally if he did not get the ice time he would like to have. I did not plan on making the same mistake I had made a year ago.

The kids took to the ice for a 5-minute warmup. As they ran through their standard drills, I watched our opponents putting on a high-speed skills clinic and again wondered whether we could pull this off. The game began, our players stuck with the plan, and we quickly realized that we were holding our own, even though the other team, as expected, had the better offensive chances. At the end of the first period, the score was 0-0. At the bench between periods, we heard the Carroll coach yelling at his players and I made sure that the kids paid attention to it. I congratulated them on their performance during first period and reminded them to stick with the plan.

Carroll scored midway through the second period to take a 1-0 lead. Surprisingly, no one panicked. Following two quick shots and saves by their goalie, I told the kids on the bench to give the line one more chance before we changed. The third opportunity was the charm. We were tied 1-1 after two periods.

As we prepared for the third period, everyone remained relaxed on the bench. My only words were "Keep playing your game." Meanwhile, our opponent's coach was now screaming at his players as he implored them to put us away. It was a scene reminiscent of the *Rocky* movie when Apollo Creed's manager yelled at him to "put this bum away and let's go home." Our kids were all gaining confidence by the minute. Although ice time was not balanced among our skaters, no one complained because they all realized that they were contributing in their own way. Everyone was following the game plan to a tee, and we were one 15-minute period away from the upset of the new millennium.

We broke the tie with just over 3 minutes left. The opposing team called time out. We knew that we were about to face an onslaught and that it would take disciplined and calm play to get out alive. As expected, they threw everything at us and tied the game with just over 2 minutes left. I called a time out and let the kids know that we had achieved one of our goals, which was to stay close in score. Now we were in a position to steal the game if we didn't change our plan.

Both teams played cautiously through the end of the final period, and we returned to the locker room as the ice was resurfaced for sudden death overtime. Our locker room scene was incredible. The kids were relaxed and joking as I reminded them that all the pressure in the world was on the team in the other locker room. "They are scared to death," I told them. Before returning to the ice, I started to explain to the kids that we would be dropping back to our top two lines. Before I could finish, our team captain, who was a third-line player, interrupted politely to let me know that everyone was on board with the decision and that he did not even care whether he saw the ice in overtime in order to win. The rest of the less-skilled players concurred.

As we went back to the bench, I was nervous because we had had another team on the ropes a year earlier and let them escape with a late regulation goal and then one in overtime. If I managed to coach two consecutive sudden death losses, it might be my epitaph. I relaxed by reminding myself that I did not have to agonize over shortening the bench. This was the second chance I wanted, and I intended to do it right.

Our first line started the overtime period, and after a short shift by the second line, I went back to our top line. As in the second period, I again decided to leave our top line on the ice to take the draw to the right of the Carroll net. I knew that we would have to score sooner rather than later because it was only a matter of time before Carroll would wear us down with their skill in the overtime situation.

The puck was dropped by the referee. Our player pushed the puck toward the open area about 10 feet in front of the net and waited for his brother to block the goalkeeper's view. Then he flipped a low, backhand shot toward the goal. Standing on the bench at the far end of the rink, none of us saw the puck enter the net. However, we did not need to see it because our players on the ice were screaming, the referee was pointing at the net to confirm the goal, and the opposing players had their heads down. The elation on our bench was indescribable as we made our way to the jubilant pile of our team in their powder blue and navy blue uniforms at the other end of the rink.

As we lined up for the traditional postgame handshake, reality had not yet set in for either team. We asked one another whether it had really happened; the other team hoped it was only a bad dream.

That year we got it right: a perfect game plan, a successful sale to the team, and the improbable of all wins. Two days later, our opponent's Web site talked about a great year coming to a sad end at the hands of our late-season magic. I now realize that our magic, like that of the 1980 U.S. Olympics team, followed these three axioms:

He who is well prepared
    and lies in wait for an enemy who is not well prepared will win.
Throw them into a situation
    where there is no escape and they will display immortal courage.
He who understands
    how to handle both superior and inferior forces will win.

KEEP YOUR WORD

T. Allen Pannell, Jr.
Management Consultant

So if it be demonstrated that the rules are customary
and reliable, all will be able to cooperate harmoniously.
—Sun Tzu

It was the worldwide kickoff meeting for a new major corporate initiative. The top 200 managers of a $1 billion family-owned business were present. In the room was the founder of the organization and the son of the founder, who was the current president. The founder was active on the board but did not deal with ongoing management issues. He was aware of, and supported, the new initiative, but not at a detail level.

I was the leader of the consulting team chosen to help implement the initiative. I was presenting the findings of an assessment instrument we had sent to the organization. Because of time constraints, the assessment had been mailed before we had the opportunity of personally discussing purpose and confidentiality with each key manager. Written instructions outlined the purpose and made a clear promise of confidentiality in order to ensure participation.

At a macrolevel, I was illustrating the variations in response from the managers' 50 locations. Four locations were selected to demonstrate the variations. In order to maintain confidentiality, I named the locations A, B, C, and D. Location C was at a point on the visual that was "not good." At the moment I presented this fact, I was making eye contact with the right-hand side of the large audience.

A voice from the left (behind me) asked, "Which location is C?" Before looking to see who asked the question, I began to answer and turned to the left, saying, "I can't tell you that because we promised confidentiality." The people to whom we made the promise are in the room. By the time I completed my response and turned around, I realized that the questioner was the founder of the company. He, of course, was unaware of the detail of the assessment and the commitment of confidentiality. Of course, he was also interested in which one of his locations was not good.

The room fell silent, and the atmosphere was quite tense. The founder repeated his question and explained why it was important for him to know. He also reminded me that he signed the checks for consultants.

Now came the moment of truth. Sun Tzu says it well, "The commander adept in war enhances the moral influence and adheres to the laws and regulations. Thus, it is in his power to control success." I knew that the only way I could have any moral influence was to be true to my word.

I repeated that I would not reveal the name of location, and why. The founder was not pleased. Our contact called for a break in the meeting to relieve the tension. During the break, the son of the founder (the president), came up to me and shook my hand. He said that one of the main pillars of the new initiative was integrity, and that I had just demonstrated it very well. He said he would handle the founder, and we moved on.

The initiative went on to be extremely successful monetarily and culturally. The president is still a fan. The founder still refers to me with profanity. I take it as a compliment.

Had I broken the commitment, I would have lost the troops, the 200 core managers, and eventually lost the contract. If I had not kept faith with the right "moral influence," there would have been no sale.

SUCCESS AT THE HIGH GROUND

Terry Gautsch
Fortune 100 Sales Manager

An important strategic advantage repeatedly stressed by Sun Tzu is to take (and hold) the high ground. It is no surprise that this concept is directly connected to sales success.

The organization holding the high ground of positive business ethics is on the right road to success. This moral level must be present throughout the corporation and exemplified by the front-line sales professionals. The ethical high ground makes it easier to get the critical first order and develop lasting relationships.

During my career in sales and marketing, I experienced the importance of this concept. I had the good fortune to be associated with a large, competent company that enjoyed a positive market image.

The perception of good business ethics combined with business competence often provided the decisive edge in making the sale.

If a company was searching for a single source partner, our reputation always placed us as the leading contender. If the customer was multisource, we were one of the leading sources.

If a product quality problem occurred, the perception of being on the ethical and quality high ground provided us the opportunity to correct the problem and continue serving the customer.

I recall a particularly thorny product problem with a major customer—the quantity of suspect product, the nature of the problem, and the potential consequences seemed monumental. Our salesperson requested a meeting with the customer's top quality and purchasing people. He presented the problem details, proposed fix, and timetable for corrective action.

We were ultimately provided the opportunity and time to correct the problem. Had we been a marginal supplier without the high ground of business ethics and competence, the situation might have been different.

Another example involved a small company that had developed a significantly improved product to compete in a mature market. To bring this new product to market, the company needed a trusted, knowledgeable component source.

After a series of negotiations revolving around the tenets of Sun Tzu's high-ground strategy, we were awarded an exclusive contract. As the product became more successful, we retained a major share of the business because the customer perceived that we were a high-ground supplier.

Clearly, the high ground strategy is very fragile and achieved only over time. One unethical sales representative can cause you to surrender the high ground no matter how worthy you are as a supplier. The road down from the high ground is much swifter than the road up.

A corollary is that the highly ethical salesperson working the high ground can achieve success with mediocre suppliers. The sales representative who is timely, follows through, adds value, and has strong ethical relationships owns his or her personal high ground.

With today's business battlefield littered with corporations that achieved a fictional high ground, it is more imperative that business and personal ethics be beyond reproach. Sales success achieved without occupying the high ground will be short-lived. Long-term success comes to those who sustain the right to occupy the moral high ground.

BOOK TWO

THE ART OF WAR
BY
SUN TZU

*Following is one of the few authentic translations
into English by Chinese nationals.
The authors of this book have inserted subheadings into each
chapter to aid in reading the timeless wisdom.*

Translated by Pan Jiabin and Liu Ruixiang,
People's Republic of China

The Lesson of the Concubines

The following story is considered to be of dubious authenticity and not part of the 13 chapters. Some translators include it within their books; others ignore its existence. You might find interesting lessons in this version.

Sun Tzu's book, The Art of War, *earned him an audience with the King of Wu who said, "I have thoroughly read your thirteen chapters. May I submit your theory of managing soldiers to a small test?"*

Sun Tzu replied, "Sir, you may."

The King of Wu asked, "Can the test be applied to women?"

Sun Tzu replied that it could, so arrangements were made to bring 180 beautiful women from the palace. Sun Tzu divided them into two companies with one of the King's favorite concubines at the head of each. He then made all of them take spears in their hands and spoke to them: "I presume you know the difference between front and back, right hand and left hand?"

The women replied, "Yes."

Sun Tzu continued, "When the drums signal 'eyes front,' you must look straight ahead. When the drums signal 'left turn,' you must face toward your left hand. When the drums signal 'right turn,' you must face toward your right hand. When the drums signal 'about turn,' you must face around to the back."

After the words of command had been explained the women agreed they understood. He gave them spears so he could begin the drill. When he used the sound of the drums to give the order 'right turn,' the women burst out in laughter.

With great patience, Sun Tzu said, "If the instructions and words of command are not clear and distinct, if orders are not thoroughly understood, then the general is to blame." He then repeated the explanations several times. This time he ordered the drums to signal 'left turn,' and again the women burst into laughter.

Then Sun Tzu said, "If the instructions and words of command are not clear and distinct, if orders are not thoroughly understood, the general is to blame. But if commands are clear and the soldiers disobey, then it is the fault of the officers." He immediately ordered the women who were leaders of the two companies to be beheaded."

Of course, the king was watching from a raised pavilion, and when he saw that his two favorite concubines were about to be executed, he was alarmed and swiftly sent down a message: "We are now quite satisfied as to the general's ability to manage troops. Without these concubines, my food and drink will not taste good. It is the king's wish that they not be beheaded."

Sun Tzu replied, "Having received the sovereign's commission to take charge and direct these troops, there are certain orders I cannot accept." He immediately had the two concubines beheaded as an example and appointed the two next in line as the new leaders.

Now the drums were sounded again and the drill began. The women performed all the maneuvers exactly as commanded, turning to the right or left, marching ahead, turning around, kneeling, or rising. They drilled perfectly in precision and did not utter a single sound.

Sun Tzu sent a messenger to the King of Wu saying, "Your Majesty, the soldiers are now correctly drilled and perfectly disciplined. They are ready for your inspection. Put them to any use you desire. As sovereign, you may choose to require them to go through fire and water and they will not disobey."

The king responded, "Our commander should cease the drill and return to his camp. We do not wish to come down and inspect the troops."

With great calm, Sun Tzu said, "This king is only fond of words and cannot carry them into deeds."

Commentary following the story indicates that the King relented, recognized Sun Tzu's ability, appointed him a general and Sun Tzu won many battles. In contrast, some historians believe Sun Tzu simply served as a civilian strategist.

The moral of the story could be a lesson on training, discipline, command structure, role playing, or persuasion. The thoughtful reader should use his or her imagination to determine applicable lessons.

Chapter 1
Laying Plans

Make a Thorough Assessment

War is a matter of vital importance to the state, a matter of life and death, the road to either survival or ruin. Hence, it is imperative that it be thoroughly studied.

Therefore, to make an assessment of the outcome of a war, one must compare the various conditions of the antagonistic sides in terms of the five constant factors:

Moral influence
Weather
Terrain
Commander
Doctrine

These five constant factors should be familiar to every general. He who masters them wins; he who does not is defeated.

Compare Attributes

Therefore, to forecast the outcome of a war, the attributes of the antagonistic sides should be analyzed by making the following seven comparisons:

Which sovereign possesses greater moral influence?
Which commander is more capable?
Which side holds more favorable conditions in weather
    and terrain?

On which side are decrees better implemented?
Which side is superior in arms?
On which side are officers and men better trained?
Which side is stricter and more impartial in meting out
rewards and punishments?

By means of these seven elements, I can forecast victory
or defeat.

If the sovereign heeds these stratagems of mine and acts
upon them, he will surely win the war, and I shall, therefore,
stay with him. If the sovereign neither heeds nor acts upon
them, he will certainly suffer defeat, and I shall leave.

Tip the Scales

Having paid attention to the advantages of my stratagems,
the commander must create a helpful situation over and
beyond the ordinary rules. By *situation* I mean he should act
expediently in accordance with what is advantageous in the
field and so meet any exigency.

All warfare is based on deception. Therefore, when able
to attack, we must pretend to be unable; when employing
our forces, we must seem inactive; when we are near, we
must make the enemy believe we are far away; when far
away, we must make him believe we are near.

Offer a bait to allure the enemy when he covets small
advantages; strike the enemy when he is in disorder. If he
is well prepared with substantial strength, take double
precautions against him. If he is powerful in action, evade
him. If he is angry, seek to discourage him. If he appears
humble, make him arrogant. If his forces have taken a
good rest, wear them down. If his forces are united, divide
them.

Launch the attack where he is unprepared; take action when it is unexpected.

These are the keys to victory for a strategist. However, it is impossible to formulate them in detail beforehand.

Now, the commander who gets many scores during the calculations in the temple before the war will have more likelihood of winning. The commander who gets few scores during the calculations in the temple before the war will have less chance of success. With many scores, one can win; with few scores, one cannot. How much less chance of victory has one who gets no scores at all! By examining the situation through these aspects, I can foresee who is likely to win or lose.

Chapter 2

Waging War

Marshal Adequate Resources

Generally, operations of war involve one thousand swift chariots, one thousand heavy chariots, and one hundred thousand mailed troops with the transportation of provisions for them over a thousand *li*. Thus, the expenditure at home and in the field, the stipends for the entertainment of state guests and diplomatic envoys, the cost of materials such as glue and lacquer, and the expense for care and maintenance of chariots and armor, will amount to one thousand pieces of gold a day. An army of one hundred thousand men can be raised only when this money is in hand.

Time and Timing Aid Victory

In directing such an enormous army, a speedy victory is the main object.

If the war is long delayed, the men's weapons will be blunted and their ardor will be dampened. If the army attacks cities, their strength will be exhausted. Again, if the army engages in protracted campaigns, the resources of the state will not suffice. Now, when your weapons are blunted, your ardor dampened, your strength exhausted, and your treasure spent, neighboring rulers will take advantage of your distress to act. In this case, no man, however wise, is able to avert the disastrous consequences that ensue.

Thus, while we have heard of stupid haste in war, we have not yet seen a clever operation that was prolonged. There has never been a case in which a prolonged war has benefited a country. Therefore, only those who understand the dangers inherent in employing troops know how to conduct war in the most profitable way.

Be Efficient

Those adept in employing troops do not require a second levy of conscripts or more than two provisionings. They carry military supplies from the homeland and make up for their provisions by relying on the enemy. Thus, the army will be always plentifully provided.

When a country is impoverished by military operations, it is because an army far from its homeland needs a distant transportation. Being forced to carry supplies for great distances renders the people destitute. On the other hand, the local price of commodities normally rises high in the area near the military camps. The rising prices cause financial resources to be drained away. When the resources are exhausted, the peasantry will be afflicted with urgent exactions. With this depletion of strength and exhaustion of wealth, every household in the homeland is left empty. Seven-tenths of the people's income is dissipated and six-tenths of the government's revenue is paid for broken-down chariots, worn-out horses, armor and helmets, arrows and crossbows, halberds and bucklers, spears and body shields, draft oxen, and heavy wagons.

Hence, a wise general is sure of getting provisions from the enemy countries. One *zhong* of grains obtained from the local area is equal to twenty *zhong* shipped from the home country; one *dan* of fodder in the conquered area is equal to twenty *dan* from the domestic store.

Gain Strength from Victory

Now in order to kill the enemy, our men must be roused to anger; to gain enemy's property, our men must be rewarded with war trophies. Accordingly, in chariot battle, when more than ten chariots have been captured, those who took the enemy chariot first should be rewarded. Then, the enemy's flags and banners should be replaced with ours; the captured chariots should be mixed with ours and mounted by our men. The prisoners of war should be kindly treated and kept. This is called *becoming stronger in the course of defeating the enemy.*

Know Your Profession

Hence, what is valued in war is a quick victory, not prolonged operations. And therefore the general who understands war is the controller of his people's fate and the guarantor of the security of the nation.

Chapter 3
Attack by Stratagem

Win without Fighting

Generally, in war the best thing of all is to take the enemy's state whole and intact; to ruin it is inferior to this. To capture the enemy's entire army is better than to destroy it; to take intact a battalion, a company, or a five-man squad is better than to destroy them. Hence, to win one hundred victories in one hundred battles is not the acme of skill. To subdue the enemy without fighting is the supreme excellence.

Thus, the best policy in war is to attack the enemy's strategy.

The second-best way is to disrupt his alliances through diplomatic means.

The next-best method is to attack his army in the field.

The worst policy is to attack walled cities. Attacking cities is the last resort when there is no alternative.

It takes at least three months to make mantlets and shielded vehicles ready and prepare necessary arms and equipment. It takes at least another three months to pile up earthen mounds against the walls. The general unable to control his impatience will order his troops to swarm up the wall like ants with the result that one-third of them are slain, while the cities remain untaken. Such is the calamity of attacking walled cities.

Therefore, those skilled in war subdue the enemy's army without fighting. They capture the enemy's cities without assaulting them and overthrow his state without protracted operations.

Their aim must be to take all under heaven intact through strategic superiority. Thus, their troops are not worn out and their triumph will be complete. This is the art of attacking by stratagem.

Get the Odds in Your Favor

Consequently, the art of using troops is this:

> When ten to the enemy's one, surround him.
> When five times his strength, attack him.
> If double his strength, engage him.
> If equally matched, be capable of dividing him.
> If less in number, be capable of defending yourself.
> And if in all respects unfavorable, be capable of eluding him.

Hence, a weak force will eventually fall captive to a strong one if it simply holds ground and conducts a desperate defense.

Beware of High-Level Weakness

Now, the general is the bulwark of the state:

> If the bulwark is complete at all points, the state will surely be strong.
> If the bulwark is defective, the state will certainly be weak.

Now, there are three ways in which a sovereign can bring misfortune upon his army:

By ordering an advance while ignorant of the fact that the army cannot go forward, or by ordering a retreat while ignorant of the fact that the army cannot fall back. This is described as hobbling the army.

By interfering with the army's administration without knowledge of the internal affairs of the army. This causes officers and soldiers to be perplexed.

By interfering with direction of fighting, while ignorant of the military principle of adaptation to circumstances. This sows doubts and misgivings in the minds of his officers and soldiers.

If the army is confused and suspicious, neighboring rulers will take advantage of this and cause trouble. This is simply bringing anarchy into the army and flinging victory away.

Seek Circumstances That Ensure Victory

Thus, there are five points by which victory may be predicted:

He who knows when to fight and when not to fight will win.

He who understands how to handle both superior and inferior forces will win.

He whose ranks are united in purpose will win.

He who is well prepared and lies in wait for an enemy who is not well prepared will win.

He whose generals are able and not interfered with by the sovereign will win.

It is in these five points that the way to victory is known. Therefore, I say:

Know the enemy and know yourself, and you
   can fight a hundred battles with no danger of
   defeat.
When you are ignorant of the enemy but know
   yourself, your chances of winning and losing
   are equal.
If ignorant both of your enemy and of yourself,
   you are sure to be defeated in every battle.

Chapter 4

Disposition of Military Strength

Be Invincible

The skillful warriors in ancient times first made themselves invincible and then awaited the enemy's moment of vulnerability. Invincibility depends on oneself, but the enemy's vulnerability depends on himself. It follows that those skilled in war can make themselves invincible but cannot cause an enemy to be certainly vulnerable. Therefore, it can be said that one may know how to achieve victory but cannot necessarily do so.

Invincibility lies in the defense; the possibility of victory, in the attack. Defend yourself when the enemy's strength is abundant; and attack the enemy when it is inadequate.

Those who are skilled in defense hide themselves as under the most secret recesses of earth.

Those skilled in attack flash forth as from above the topmost heights of heaven.

Thus, they are capable both of protecting themselves and of gaining a complete victory.

Get Your Strategy Right

To foresee a victory no better than ordinary people's foresight is not the acme of excellence. Neither is it the acme of excellence if you win a victory through fierce fighting and the whole empire says, "Well done!" Hence, by analogy, to lift an autumn hair [hare] does not signify great strength; to see the sun and moon does not signify good sight; to hear the thunderclap does not signify acute hearing.

In ancient times, those called skilled in war conquered an enemy easily conquered. Consequently, a master of war wins victories without showing his brilliant military success, and without gaining the reputation for wisdom or the merit for valor. He wins his victories without making mistakes. Making no mistakes is what establishes the certainty of victory, for it means that he conquers an enemy already defeated.

Accordingly, a wise commander always ensures that his forces are put in an invincible position, and at the same time will be sure to miss no opportunity to defeat the enemy. It follows that a triumphant army will not fight with the enemy until the victory is assured, while an army destined to defeat will always fight with the opponent first, in the hope that it may win by sheer good luck. The commander adept in war enhances the moral influence and adheres to the laws and regulations. Thus, it is in his power to control success.

Lead from Strength

Now, the elements of the art of war are first, the measurement of space; second, the estimation of quantities; third, the calculation of figures; fourth, comparisons of strength; and fifth, chances of victory.

Measurements of space are derived from the ground. Quantities derive from measurement, figures from quantities, comparisons from figures, and victory from comparisons.

Therefore, a victorious army is as one *yi* balanced against a grain, and a defeated army is as a grain balanced against one *yi*.

An army superior in strength takes action like the bursting of pent-up waters into a chasm of a thousand fathoms deep. This is what the disposition of military strength means in the actions of war.

Chapter 5

Use of Energy

Generally, management of a large force is the same in principle as the management of a few men: It is a matter of organization. And to direct a large army to fight is the same as to direct a small one: It is a matter of command signs and signals.

Do the Extraordinary

That the whole army can sustain the enemy's all-out attack without suffering defeat is due to operations of extraordinary and normal forces. Troops thrown against the enemy as a grindstone against eggs is an example of the strong beating the weak.

Generally, in battle, use the normal force to engage and use the extraordinary to win. Now, to a commander adept at the use of extraordinary forces, his resources are as infinite as the heaven and earth, as inexhaustible as the flow of the running rivers. They end and begin again like the motions of the sun and moon. They die away and then are reborn like the changing of the four seasons.

In battle, there are not more than two kinds of postures—operation of the extraordinary force and operation of the normal force—but their combinations give rise to an endless series of maneuvers. For these two forces are mutually reproductive. It is like moving in a circle, never coming to an end. Who can exhaust the possibilities of their combinations?

Unleash the Power of Timing and Momentum

When torrential water tosses boulders, it is because of its momentum; when the strike of a hawk breaks the body of its prey, it is because of timing. Thus, in battle, a good commander creates a posture releasing an irresistible and overwhelming momentum, and his attack is precisely timed in a quick tempo. The energy is similar to a fully drawn crossbow—the timing, the release of the trigger.

Have a System to Release Energy

Amid the turmoil and tumult of battle, there may be seeming disorder and yet no real disorder in one's own troops. In the midst of confusion and chaos, your troops appear to be milling about in circles, yet it is proof against defeat.

Apparent disorder is born of order; apparent cowardice, of courage; apparent weakness, of strength. Order or disorder depends on organization and direction; courage or cowardice, on postures; strength or weakness, on dispositions.

Thus, one who is adept at keeping the enemy on the move maintains deceitful appearances, according to which the enemy will act. He lures with something that the enemy is certain to take. By so doing he keeps the enemy on the move and then waits for the right moment to make a sudden ambush with picked troops.

Therefore, a skilled commander sets great store by using the situation to the best advantage, and does not make excessive demands on his subordinates. Hence he is able to select the right men and exploits the situation. He who takes advantage of the situation uses his men in fighting as rolling logs or rocks. It is the nature of logs and rocks to stay stationary on the flat ground, and to roll forward on a slope. If four-cornered, they stop; if round-shaped, they roll. Thus, the energy of troops skillfully commanded is just like the momentum of round rocks quickly tumbling down from a mountain thousands of feet in height. This is what *use of energy* means.

Chapter 6
Weakness and Strength

Seize the Initiative

Generally, he who occupies the field of battle first and awaits his enemy is at ease; he who arrives later and joins battle in haste is weary. And, therefore, one skilled in war brings the enemy to the field of battle and is not brought there by him.

One able to make the enemy come of his own accord does so by offering him some advantage. And one able to stop him from coming does so by inflicting damage on him.

Achieve Surprise

Thus, when the enemy is at ease, he is able to tire him; when well fed, to starve him; when at rest, to make him move. All these can be done because you appear at points which the enemy must hasten to defend.

That you may march a thousand *li* without tiring yourself is because you travel where there is no enemy.

That you are certain to take what you attack is because you attack a place the enemy does not or cannot protect.

That you are certain of success in holding what you defend is because you defend a place the enemy must hasten to attack.

Therefore, against those skillful in attack, the enemy does not know where to defend, and against the experts in defense, the enemy does not know where to attack.

How subtle and insubstantial that the expert leaves no trace. How divinely mysterious that he is inaudible. Thus, he is master of his enemy's fate.

His offensive will be irresistible if he plunges into the enemy's weak points; he cannot be overtaken when he withdraws if he moves swiftly. Hence, if we wish to fight, the enemy will be compelled to an engagement even though he is safe behind high ramparts and deep ditches. This is because we attack a position he must relieve.

If we do not wish to fight, we can prevent him from engaging us even though the lines of our encampment be merely traced out on the ground. This is because we divert him from going where he wishes.

Be a Gorilla—or Be a Guerrilla

Accordingly, by exposing the enemy's dispositions and remaining invisible ourselves, we can keep our forces concentrated, while the enemy's must be divided. We can form a single united body at one place, while the enemy must scatter his forces at ten places. Thus, it is ten to one when we attack him at one place, which means we are numerically superior. And if we are able to use many to strike few at the selected place, those we deal with will be in dire straits.

The spot where we intend to fight must not be made known. In this way, the enemy must take precautions at many places against the attack. The more places he must guard, the fewer his troops we shall have to face at any given point.

For if he prepares to the front, his rear will be weak; and if to the rear, his front will be fragile. If he strengthens his left, his right will be vulnerable; and if his right gets strengthened, there will be few troops on his left. If he sends reinforcements everywhere, he will be weak everywhere.

Numerical weakness comes from having to prepare against possible attacks; numerical strength, from compelling the enemy to make these preparations against us.

Understand Strong and Weak Points

Therefore, if one knows the place and time of the coming battle, his troops can march a thousand *li* and fight on the field. But if one knows neither the spot nor the time, then one cannot manage to have the left wing help the right wing or the right wing help the left; the forces in the front will be unable to support the rear, and the rear will be unable to reinforce the front. How much more so if the furthest portions of the troop deployments extend tens of *li* in breadth, and even the nearest troops are separated by several *li*!

Although I estimate the troops of Yue as many, of what benefit is this superiority in terms of victory?

Thus, I say that victory can be achieved. For even if the enemy is numerically stronger, we can prevent him from fighting.

Therefore, analyze the enemy's battle plan, so as to have a clear understanding of its strong and weak points. Agitate the enemy so as to ascertain his pattern of movement. Lure him into the open so as to find out his vulnerable spots in disposition. Probe him and learn where his strength is abundant and where deficient.

Now, the ultimate in disposing one's troops is to conceal them without ascertainable shape. In this way, the most penetrating spies cannot pry nor can the wise lay plans against you.

Use Flexible Tactics

Even though we show people the victory gained by using flexible tactics in conformity to the changing situations, they do not comprehend this. People all know the tactics by which we achieved victory, but they do not know how the tactics were applied in the situation to defeat the enemy. Hence no one victory is gained in the same manner as another. The tactics change in an infinite variety of ways to suit changes in the circumstances.

Now, the laws of military operations are like water. The tendency of water is to flow from heights to lowlands. The law of successful operations is to avoid the enemy's strength and strike his weakness. Water changes its course in accordance with the contours of the land. The soldier works out his victory in accordance with the situation of the enemy.

Hence, there are neither fixed postures nor constant tactics in warfare. He who can modify his tactics in accordance with the enemy situation and thereby succeeds in winning may be said to be divine. Of the five elements, none is ever predominant; of the four seasons, none lasts forever; of the days, some are longer and others shorter; and of the moon, it sometimes waxes and sometimes wanes.

Chapter 7

Maneuvering

Maneuver Can Create Advantages

Normally, in war, the general receives his commands from the sovereign. During the process from assembling the troops and mobilizing the people to deploying the army ready for battle, nothing is more difficult than the art of maneuvering for seizing favorable positions beforehand. What is difficult about it is to make the devious route the most direct and to turn disadvantage to advantage. Thus, forcing the enemy to deviate and slow down his march by luring him with a bait, you may set out after he does and arrive at the battlefield before him. One able to do this shows knowledge of the artifice of deviation.

Thus, both advantage and danger are inherent in maneuvering for an advantageous position. One who sets the entire army in motion with impedimenta to pursue an advantageous position will be too slow to attain it. If he abandons the camp and all the impedimenta to contend for advantage, the baggage and stores will be lost.

It follows that when the army rolls up the armor and sets out speedily, stopping neither day nor night and marching at double speed for a hundred *li* to wrest an advantage, the commander of three divisions will be captured. The vigorous troops will arrive first and the feeble will straggle along behind, so that if this method is used, only one-tenth of the army will arrive. In a forced march of fifty *li* the commander of the first and van division will fall, and using this method but half of the army will arrive. In a forced march of thirty *li*, but two-thirds will arrive. Hence, the army will be lost without the baggage train; and it cannot survive without provisions, nor can it last long without sources of supplies.

Keep Out of the Swamp

One who is not acquainted with the designs of his neighbors should not enter into alliances with them. Those who do not know the conditions of mountains and forests, hazardous defiles, marshes and swamps cannot conduct the march of an army. Those who do not use local guides are unable to obtain the advantages of the ground.

Mislead Your Opponent

Now, war is based on deception. Move when it is advantageous and change tactics by dispersal and concentration of your troops. When campaigning, be swift as the wind; in leisurely march, be majestic as the forest; in raiding and plundering, be fierce as fire; in standing, be firm as the mountains. When hiding, be as unfathomable as things behind the clouds; when moving, fall like a thunderclap. When you plunder the countryside, divide your forces. When you conquer territory, defend strategic points.

Weigh the situation before you move. He who knows the artifice of deviation will be victorious. Such is the art of maneuvering.

Lead a Winning Team

The Book of Army Management says: "As the voice cannot be heard in battle, gongs and drums are used. As troops cannot see each other clearly in battle, flags and banners are used."

Hence, in night fighting, usually use drums and gongs; in day fighting, banners and flags. Now, these instruments are used to unify the action of the troops. When the troops can be thus united, the brave cannot advance alone, nor can the cowardly retreat. This is the art of directing large masses of troops.

A whole army may be robbed of its spirit, and its commander deprived of his presence of mind. Now, at the beginning of a campaign, the spirit of soldiers is keen; after a certain period of time, it declines; and in the later stage, it may be dwindled to naught. A clever commander, therefore, avoids the enemy when his spirit is keen and attacks him when it is lost. This is the art of attaching importance to moods. In good order, he awaits a disorderly enemy; in serenity, a clamorous one. This is the art of retaining self-possession. Close to the field of battle, he awaits an enemy coming from afar; at rest, he awaits an exhausted enemy; with well fed-troops, he awaits hungry ones. This is the art of husbanding one's strength.

He refrains from intercepting an enemy whose banners are in perfect order, and desists from attacking an army whose formations are in an impressive array. This is the art of assessing circumstances.

Now, the art of employing troops is that when the enemy occupies high ground, do not confront him uphill, and when his back is resting on hills, do not make a frontal attack. When he pretends to flee, do not pursue. Do not attack soldiers whose temper is keen. Do not swallow a bait offered by the enemy. Do not thwart an enemy who is returning homewards. When you surround an army, leave an outlet free. Do not press a desperate enemy too hard. Such is the method of using troops.

Chapter 8

Variation of Tactics

Vary Your Tactics

Generally, in war, the general receives his commands from the sovereign, assembles troops, and mobilizes the people. When on grounds hard of access, do not encamp. On grounds intersected with highways, join hands with your allies. Do not linger on critical ground. In encircled ground, resort to stratagem. In desperate ground, fight a last-ditch battle.

There are some roads which must not be followed, some troops which must not be attacked, some cities which must not be assaulted, some ground which must not be contested, and some commands of the sovereign which must not be obeyed.

Hence, the general who thoroughly understands the advantages that accompany variation of tactics knows how to employ troops.

The general who does not is unable to use the terrain to his advantage even though he is well acquainted with it. In employing the troops for attack, the general who does not understand the variation of tactics will be unable to use them effectively, even if he is familiar with the five constant advantages.

Consider Favorable and Unfavorable Factors

And for this reason, a wise general in his deliberations must consider both favorable and unfavorable factors. By taking into account the favorable factors, he makes his plan feasible; by taking into account the unfavorable, he may avoid possible disasters.

What can subdue the hostile neighboring rulers is to hit what hurts them most; what can keep them constantly occupied is to make trouble for them; and what can make them rush about is to offer them ostensible allurements.

It is a doctrine of war that we must not rely on the likelihood of the enemy not coming, but on our own readiness to meet him, not on the chance of his not attacking, but on the fact that we have made our position invincible.

Avoid the Faults of Leadership

There are five dangerous faults which may affect a general:

> If reckless, he can be killed.
> If cowardly, he can be captured.
> If quick-tempered, he can be provoked to rage and make a fool of himself.
> If he has too delicate a sense of honor, he is liable to fall into a trap because of an insult.
> If he is of a compassionate nature, he may get bothered and upset.

These are the five serious faults of a general, ruinous to the conduct of war. The ruin of the army and the death of the general are inevitable results of these five dangerous faults. They must be deeply pondered.

Chapter 9

On the March

Seek the Strength of Natural Positions

Generally, when an army takes up a position and sizes up the enemy situation, it should pay attention to the following:

When crossing the mountains, be sure to stay in the neighborhood of valleys; when encamping, select high ground facing the sunny side; when high ground is occupied by the enemy, do not ascend to attack. So much for taking up a position in mountains.

After crossing a river, you should get far away from it. When an advancing invader crosses a river, do not meet him in midstream. It is advantageous to allow half his force to get across and then strike. If you wish to fight a battle, you should not go to meet the invader near a river which he has to cross. When encamping in the riverine area, take a position on high ground facing the sun. Do not take a position at the lower reaches of the enemy. This relates to positions near a river.

In crossing salt marshes, your sole concern should be to get over them quickly, without any delay. If you encounter the enemy in a salt marsh, you should take position close to grass and water with trees to your rear. This has to do with taking up a position in salt marshes.

On level ground, take up an accessible position and deploy your main flanks on high grounds with the front lower than the back. This is how to take up a position on level ground. These are principles for encamping in the four situations named. By employing them, the Yellow Emperor conquered his four neighboring sovereigns.

Occupy the High Ground

Generally, in battle and maneuvering, all armies prefer high ground to low, and sunny places to shady. If an army encamps close to water and grass with adequate supplies, it will be free from countless diseases and this will spell victory. When you come to hills, dikes, or embankments, occupy the sunny side, with your main flank at the back. All these methods are advantageous to the army and can exploit the possibilities the ground offers.

When heavy rain falls in the upper reaches of a river and foaming water descends, do not ford but wait until it subsides. When encountering Precipitous Torrents, Heavenly Wells, Heavenly Prison, Heavenly Net, Heavenly Trap, and Heavenly Cracks, you must march speedily away from them. Do not approach them. While we keep a distance from them, we should draw the enemy toward them. We face them and cause the enemy to put his back to them.

If in the neighborhood of your camp there are dangerous defiles or ponds and low-lying ground overgrown with aquatic grass and reeds, or forested mountains with dense, tangled undergrowth, they must be thoroughly searched, for these are possible places where ambushes are laid and spies are hidden.

Observe What Is Happening

When the enemy is close at hand and remains quiet, he is relying on a favorable position. When he challenges battle from afar, he wishes to lure you to advance; when he is on easy ground, he must be in an advantageous position. When the trees are seen to move, it means the enemy is advancing; when many screens have been placed in the undergrowth, it is for the purpose of deception. The rising of birds in their flight is the sign of an ambuscade. Startled beasts indicate that a sudden attack is forthcoming.

Dust spurting upward in high straight columns indicates the approach of chariots. When it hangs low and is widespread, it betokens that infantry is approaching. When it branches out in different directions, it shows that parties have been sent out to collect firewood. A few clouds of dust moving to and fro signify that the army is camping.

When the enemy's envoys speak in humble terms, but the army continues preparations, that means it will advance. When their language is strong and the enemy pretentiously drives forward, these may be signs that he will retreat. When light chariots first go out and take positions on the wings, it is a sign that the enemy is forming for battle. When the enemy is not in dire straits but asks for a truce, he must be plotting. When his troops march speedily and parade in formations, he is expecting to fight a decisive battle on a fixed date. When half his force advances and half retreats, he is attempting to decoy you.

When his troops lean on their weapons, they are famished. When drawers of water drink before carrying it to camp, his troops are suffering from thirst. When the enemy sees an advantage but does not advance to seize it, he is fatigued.

When birds gather above his campsites, they are unoccupied. When at night the enemy's camp is clamorous, it betokens nervousness. If there is disturbance in the camp, the general's authority is weak.

If the banners and flags are shifted about, sedition is afoot. If the officers are angry, it means that men are weary. When the enemy feeds his horses with grain, kills the beasts of burden for food, and packs up the utensils used for drawing water, he shows no intention to return to his tents and is determined to fight to the death.

When the general speaks in a meek and subservient tone to his subordinates, he has lost the support of his men. Too frequent rewards indicate that the general is at the end of his resources; too frequent punishments indicate that he is in dire distress. If the officers at first treat the men violently and later are fearful of them, it shows supreme lack of intelligence.

When envoys are sent with compliments in their mouths, it is a sign that the enemy wishes for a truce.

When the enemy's troops march up angrily and remain facing yours for a long time, neither joining battle nor withdrawing, the situation demands great vigilance and thorough investigation.

In war, numbers alone confer no advantage. If one does not advance by force recklessly, and is able to concentrate his military power through a correct assessment of the enemy situation and enjoys full support of his men, that would suffice. He who lacks foresight and underestimates his enemy will surely be captured by him.

Be Fair—Generate Harmony

If troops are punished before they have grown attached to you, they will be disobedient. If troops are not obedient, it is difficult to employ them. If troops have become attached to you, but discipline is not enforced, you cannot employ them either. Thus, soldiers must be treated in the first instance with humanity, but kept under control by iron discipline. In this way, the allegiance of soldiers is assured.

If orders are consistently carried out and the troops are strictly supervised, they will be obedient. If orders are never carried out, they will be disobedient. And the smooth implementation of orders reflects harmonious relationships between the commander and his troops.

Chapter 10

Terrain

Know the Battlefield

Ground may be classified according to its nature as accessible, entangling, temporizing, constricted, precipitous, and distant.

Ground which both we and the enemy can traverse with equal ease is called *accessible*. On such ground, he who first takes high sunny positions and keeps his supply routes unimpeded can fight advantageously.

Ground easy to reach but difficult to exit is called *entangling*. The nature of this ground is such that if the enemy is unprepared and you sally out, you may defeat him. But, if the enemy is prepared for your coming, and you fail to defeat him, then, return being difficult, disadvantages will ensue.

Ground equally disadvantageous for both the enemy and ourselves to enter is called *temporizing*. The nature of this ground is such that even though the enemy should offer us an attractive bait, it will be advisable not to go forth but march off. When his force is halfway out because of our maneuvering, we can strike him with advantage.

With regard to *constricted* ground, if we first occupy it, we must block the narrow passes with strong garrisons and wait for the enemy. Should the enemy first occupy such ground, do not attack him if the pass in his hand is fully garrisoned, but only if it is weakly garrisoned.

With regard to *precipitous* ground, if we first occupy it, we must take a position on the sunny heights and await the enemy. If he first occupies such ground, we should march off and do not attack him.

When the enemy is situated at a great distance from us, and the terrain where the two armies deploy is similar, it is difficult to provoke battle and unprofitable to engage him.

These are the principles relating to six different types of ground. It is the highest responsibility of the general to inquire into them with the utmost care.

Know the Causes of Failure

There are six situations that cause an army to fail. They are flight, insubordination, fall, collapse, disorganization, and rout. None of these disasters can be attributed to natural and geographical causes, but to the fault of the general.

Terrain conditions being equal, if a force attacks one ten times its size, the result is flight.

When the soldiers are strong and officers weak, the army is insubordinate.

When the officers are valiant and the soldiers ineffective, the army will fall.

When the higher officers are angry and insubordinate, and on encountering the enemy rush to battle on their own account from a feeling of resentment and the commander in chief is ignorant of their abilities, the result is collapse.

When the general is incompetent and has little authority, when his troops are mismanaged, when the relationship between the officers and men is strained, and when the troop formations are slovenly, the result is disorganization.

When a general unable to estimate the enemy's strength uses a small force to engage a larger one or weak troops to strike the strong, or fails to select shock troops for the van, the result is rout.

When any of these six situations exists, the army is on the road to defeat. It is the highest responsibility of the general that he examine them carefully.

Know When to Fight

Conformation of the ground is of great assistance in military operations. It is necessary for a wise general to make correct assessments of the enemy's situation to create conditions leading to victory and to calculate distances and the degree of difficulty of the terrain. He who knows these things and applies them to fighting will definitely win. He who knows them not, and, therefore, is unable to apply them, will definitely lose.

Hence, if, in the light of the prevailing situation, fighting is sure to result in victory, then you may decide to fight even though the sovereign has issued an order not to engage.

If fighting does not stand a good chance of victory, you need not fight even though the sovereign has issued an order to engage.

Hence, the general who advances without coveting fame and retreats without fearing disgrace, whose only purpose is to protect his people and promote the best interests of his sovereign, is the precious jewel of the state.

Practice Good Discipline

If a general regards his men as infants, then they will march with him into the deepest valleys. He treats them as his own beloved sons, and they will stand by him unto death. If, however, a general is indulgent toward his men but cannot employ them, cherishes them but cannot command them, or inflicts punishment on them when they violate the regulations, then they may be compared to spoiled children, and are useless for any practical purpose.

Know Yourself; Know Your Opponent

If we know that our troops are capable of striking the enemy, but do not know that he is invulnerable to attack, our chance of victory is but half.

If we know that the enemy is vulnerable to attack but do not know that our troops are incapable of striking him, our chance of victory is again but half.

If we know that the enemy can be attacked and that our troops are capable of attacking him, but do not realize that the conformation of the ground makes fighting impracticable, our chance of victory is once again but half.

Therefore, when those experienced in war move, they are never bewildered; when they act, they are never at a loss. Thus the saying: "Know the enemy and know yourself, and your victory will never be endangered; know the weather and know the ground, and your victory will then be complete."

Chapter 11

The Nine Varieties of Ground

Choose the Battleground

In respect to the employment of troops, ground may be classified as dispersive, frontier, key, open, focal, serious, difficult, encircled, and desperate.

When a chieftain is fighting in his own territory, he is in dispersive ground.

When he has penetrated into hostile territory, but to no great distance, he is in frontier ground.

Ground equally advantageous for us and the enemy to occupy is key ground.

Ground equally accessible to both sides is open.

Ground contiguous to three other states is focal. He who first gets control of it will gain the support of the majority of neighboring states.

When an army has penetrated deep into hostile territory, leaving far behind many enemy cities and towns, it is in serious ground.

Mountain forests, rugged steeps, marshes, fens, and all that is hard to traverse fall into the category of difficult ground.

Ground to which access is constricted and from which we can retire only by tortuous paths so that a small number of the enemy would suffice to crush a large body of our men is encircled ground.

Ground on which the army can avoid annihilation only

through a desperate fight without delay is called a desperate one.

And, therefore,

Do not fight in dispersive ground.
Do not stop in the frontier borderlands.
Do not attack an enemy who has occupied key ground.

In open ground, do not allow your communication to be blocked.

In focal ground, form alliances with neighboring states.
In serious ground, gather in plunder.
In difficult ground, press on.
In encircled ground, resort to stratagems.
In desperate ground, fight courageously.

Disrupt Your Opponent

In ancient times, those described as skilled in war knew how to make it impossible for the enemy to unite his van and his rear, for his large and small divisions to cooperate, for his officers and men to support each other, and for the higher and lower levels of the enemy to establish contact with each other.

When the enemy's forces were dispersed, they prevented him from assembling them; even when assembled, they managed to throw his forces into disorder. They moved forward when it was advantageous to do so; when not advantageous, they halted.

Should one ask: "How do I cope with a well-ordered enemy host about to attack me?" I reply: "Seize something he cherishes and he will conform to your desires."

Find Sources of Strength

Speed is the essence of war. Take advantage of the enemy's unpreparedness, make your way by unexpected routes, and attack him where he has taken no precautions.

The general principles applicable to an invading force are that the deeper you penetrate into hostile territory, the greater will be the solidarity of your troops, and thus the defenders cannot overcome you.

Plunder fertile country to supply your army with plentiful food. Pay attention to the soldiers' well-being and do not fatigue them. Try to keep them in high spirits and conserve their energy. Keep the army moving and devise unfathomable plans.

Survival Builds Winning Teamwork

Throw your soldiers into a position whence there is no escape, and they will choose death over desertion. For if prepared to die, how can the officers and men not exert their uttermost strength to fight? In a desperate situation, they fear nothing; when there is no way out, they stand firm. Deep in a hostile land they are bound together. If there is no help for it, they will fight hard.

Thus, without waiting to be marshaled, the soldiers will be constantly vigilant; without waiting to be asked, they will do your will; without restrictions, they will be faithful; without giving orders, they can be trusted.

Prohibit superstitious practices and do away with rumors; then nobody will flee even facing death. Our soldiers have no surplus of wealth, but it is not because they disdain riches; they have no expectation of long life, but it is not because they dislike longevity.

On the day the army is ordered out to battle, your soldiers may weep, those sitting up wetting their garments and those lying down letting the tears run down their cheeks. But throw them into a situation where there is no escape and they will display the immortal courage of Zhuan Zhu and Cao Kuei.

Troops directed by a skillful general are comparable to the Shuai Ran. The Shuai Ran is a snake found in Mount Heng. Strike at its head, and you will be attacked by its tail; strike at its tail, and you will be attacked by its head; strike at its middle, and you will be attacked by both its head and its tail. Should one ask: "Can troops be made capable of such instantaneous coordination as the Shuai Ran?" I reply: "They can." For the men of Wu and the men of Yue are enemies, yet if they are crossing a river in the same boat and are caught by a storm, they will come to each other's assistance just as the left hand helps the right.

Hence, it is not sufficient to rely upon tethering of the horses and the burying of the chariots. The principle of military administration is to achieve a uniform level of courage. The principle of terrain application is to make the best use of both the high and the low-lying grounds.

Learn Winning Ways

Thus, a skillful general conducts his army just as if he were leading a single man, willy-nilly, by the hand.

It is the business of a general to be quiet and thus ensure depth in deliberation; impartial and upright and thus keep a good management.

He should be able to mystify his officers and men by false reports and appearances, and thus keep them in total ignorance. He changes his arrangements and alters his plans in order to make others unable to see through his strategies. He shifts his campsites and undertakes marches by devious routes so as to make it impossible for others to anticipate his objective.

He orders his troops for a decisive battle on a fixed date and cuts off their return route, as if he kicks away the ladder behind the soldiers when they have climbed up a height. When he leads his army deep into hostile territory, their momentum is trigger-released in battle. He drives his men now in one direction, then in another, like a shepherd driving a flock of sheep, and no one knows where he is going. To assemble the host of his army and bring it into danger—this may be termed the business of the general.

The Battlefield Determines Action

The different measures appropriate to the nine varieties of ground and the expediency of advance or withdrawal in accordance with circumstances and the fundamental laws of human nature are matters that must be studied carefully by a general.

> Generally, when invading a hostile territory, the deeper the troops penetrate, the more cohesive they will be; penetrating only a short way causes dispersion.
> When you leave your own country behind, and take your army across neighboring territory, you find yourself on critical ground.
> When there are means of communication on all four sides, it is focal ground.
> When you penetrate deeply into a country, it is serious ground.
> When you penetrate but a little way, it is frontier ground.
> When you have the enemy's strongholds on your rear, and narrow passes in front, it is encircled ground.
> When there is no place of refuge at all, it is desperate ground.

Follow the Rules Governing Victory

Therefore,

> In dispersive ground, I would unify the determination of the army.
> In frontier ground, I would keep my forces closely linked.
> In key ground, I would hasten up my rear elements.
> In open ground, I would pay close attention to my defense.
> In focal ground, I would consolidate my alliances.
> In serious ground, I would ensure a continuous flow of provisions.
> In difficult ground, I would press on over the road.
> In encircled ground, I would block the points of access and egress.
> In desperate ground, I would make it evident that there is no chance of survival. For it is the nature of soldiers to resist when surrounded, to fight hard when there is no alternative, and to follow commands implicitly when they have fallen into danger.

One ignorant of the designs of neighboring states cannot enter into alliance with them; if ignorant of the conditions of mountains, forests, dangerous defiles, swamps, and marshes, he cannot conduct the march of an army; if he fails to make use of native guides, he cannot gain the advantages of the ground.

An army does not deserve the title of the Invincible Army of the Hegemonic King if its commander is ignorant of even one of these nine varieties of ground. Now, when such an invincible army attacks a powerful state, it makes it impossible for the enemy to assemble his forces. It overawes the enemy and prevents his allies from joining him. It follows that one does not need to seek alliances with other neighboring states, nor is there any need to foster the power of other states, but only to pursue one's own strategic designs to overawe his enemy. Then one can take the enemy's cities and overthrow the enemy's state.

Bestow rewards irrespective of customary practice and issue orders irrespective of convention and you can command a whole army as though it were but one man.

Have a Plan

Set the troops to their tasks without revealing your designs. When the task is dangerous, do not tell them its advantageous aspect. Throw them into a perilous situation and they will survive; put them in desperate ground and they will live. For when the army is placed in such a situation, it can snatch victory from defeat.

Now, the key to military operations lies in cautiously studying the enemy's designs. Concentrate your forces in the main direction against the enemy, and from a distance of a thousand *li* you can kill his general. This is called the *ability to achieve one's aim in an artful and ingenious manner*.

Therefore, on the day the decision is made to launch war, you should close the passes, destroy the official tallies, and stop the passage of all emissaries. Examine the plan closely in the temple council and make final arrangements.

If the enemy leaves a door open, you must rush in. Seize the place the enemy values without making an appointment for battle with him.

Be flexible and decide your line of action according to the situation on the enemy side.

At first, then, exhibit the coyness of a maiden until the enemy gives you an opening; afterward be swift as a running hare, and it will be too late for the enemy to oppose you.

Chapter 12

Attack by Fire

Be Disruptive and Intrusive

There are five ways of attacking with fire.

First is to burn soldiers in their camp;
second, to burn provision and stores;
third, to burn baggage-trains;
fourth, to burn arsenals and magazines;
fifth, to burn the lines of transportation.

To use fire, some medium must be relied upon. Materials for setting fire must always be at hand. There are suitable seasons to attack with fire, and special days for starting a conflagration. The suitable seasons are when the weather is very dry; the special days are those when the moon is in the constellations of the Sieve, the Wall, the Wing, or the Crossbar; for when the moon is in these positions there are likely to be strong winds all day long.

Now, in attacking with fire, one must respond to the five changing situations:

When fire breaks out in the enemy's camp, immediately coordinate your action from without.
If there is an outbreak of fire, but the enemy's soldiers remain calm, bide your time and do not attack.
When the force of the flames has reached its height, follow it up with an attack, if that is practicable; if not, stay where you are.
If fires can be raised from outside the enemy's camps, it is not necessary to wait until they are started inside.

Attack with fire only when the moment is suitable. If the fire starts from upwind, do not launch attack from downwind. When the wind continues blowing during the day, then it is likely to die down at night.

Now, the army must know the five different fire-attack situations and wait for appropriate times.

Those who use fire to assist their attacks can achieve tangible results; those who use inundations can make their attacks more powerful. Water can intercept and isolate an enemy, but cannot deprive him of the supplies or equipment.

Build Long Term

Now, to win battles and capture lands and cities, but to fail to consolidate these achievements is ominous and may be described as a waste of resources and time. And, therefore, the enlightened rulers must deliberate upon the plans to go to battle, and good generals carefully execute them.

Choose Your Battles

If not in the interests of the state, do not act. If you are not sure of success, do not use troops. If you are not in danger, do not fight a battle.

A sovereign should not launch a war simply out of anger, nor should a general fight a war simply out of resentment. Take action if it is to your advantage; cancel the action if it is not. An angered man can be happy again, just as a resentful one can feel pleased again, but a state that has perished can never revive, nor can a dead man be brought back to life.

Therefore, with regard to the matter of war, the enlightened ruler is prudent, and the good general is full of caution. Thus, the state is kept secure and the army preserved.

Chapter 13

Employment of Secret Agents

Budget Adequate Funds

Generally, when an army of one hundred thousand is raised and dispatched on a distant war, the expenses borne by the people together with the disbursements made by the treasury will amount to a thousand pieces of gold per day. There will be continuous commotion both at home and abroad; people will be involved with convoys and exhausted from performing transportation services, and seven hundred thousand households will be unable to continue their farmwork.

Hostile armies confront each other for years in order to struggle for victory in a decisive battle; yet if one who begrudges the expenditure of one hundred pieces of gold in honors and emoluments remains ignorant of his enemy's situation, he is completely devoid of humanity. Such a man is no leader of the troops, no capable assistant to his sovereign, no master of victory.

Develop an Intelligence Network

Now, the reason that the enlightened sovereign and the wise general conquer the enemy whenever they move and their achievements surpass those of ordinary men is that they have foreknowledge. This foreknowledge cannot be elicited from spirits, nor from gods, nor by analogy with past events, nor by any deductive calculations. It must be obtained from the men who know the enemy situation.

Hence, the use of spies, of whom there are five sorts: native spies, internal spies, converted spies, doomed spies, and surviving spies.

When all these five sorts of spies are at work and none knows their method of operation, it would be divinely intricate and constitutes the greatest treasure of a sovereign.

Native spies are those we employ from the enemy's country people.
Internal spies are enemy officials whom we employ.
Converted spies are enemy spies whom we employ.
Doomed spies are those of our own spies who are deliberately given false information and told to report it.
Surviving spies are those who return from the enemy camp to report information.

Hence, of all those in the army close to the commander, none is more intimate than the spies; of all rewards, none more liberal than those given to spies; of all matters, none is more confidential than those relating to spying operations.

He who is not sage cannot use spies. He who is not humane and generous cannot use spies. And he who is not delicate and subtle cannot get the truth out of them. Delicate indeed! Truly delicate!

There is no place where espionage is not possible. If plans relating to spying operations are prematurely divulged, the spy and all those to whom he spoke of them should be put to death.

Generally, whether it be armies that you wish to strike, cities that you wish to attack, and individuals that you wish to assassinate, it is necessary to find out the names of the garrison commander, the aides-de-camp, the ushers, gatekeepers, and bodyguards. You must instruct your spies to ascertain these matters in minute detail.

It is essential to seek out enemy spies who have come to conduct espionage against you and bribe them to serve you. Courteously exhort them and give your instructions, then release them back home. Thus, converted spies are recruited and used. It is through the information brought by the converted spies that native and internal spies can be recruited and employed. It is owing to their information, again, that the doomed spies, armed with false information, can be sent to convey it to the enemy. Lastly, it is by their information that the surviving spies can come back and give information as scheduled. The sovereign must have full knowledge of the activities of the five sorts of spies. And to know these depends upon the converted spies. Therefore, it is mandatory that they be treated with the utmost liberality.

In ancient times, the rise of the Shang Dynasty was due to Yi Zhi, who had served under the Xia. Likewise, the rise of the Zhou Dynasty was due to Lu Ya, who had served under the Yin. Therefore, it is only the enlightened sovereign and the wise general who are able to use the most intelligent people as spies and achieve great results. Spying operations are essential in war; upon them the army relies to make its every move.

Index

INDEX

INDEX

INDEX

INDEX

INDEX